Arts Therapies with People with Physical Disabilities

of related interest

Art Therapy with Physical Conditions
Edited by Marian Liebmann and Sally Weston
Foreword by Trevor Thompson
ISBN 978 1 84905 349 5
eISBN 978 0 85700 911 1

Music Therapy for Multisensory and Body Awareness in Children and Adults with Severe to Profound Multiple Disabilities
The MuSense Manual
Roberta S. Adler and Olga V. Samsonova-Jellison
Foreword by William Cable
ISBN 978 1 78592 736 2
eISBN 978 1 78450 447 2

Developmental Drama
Dramatherapy Approaches for People with Profound or Severe Multiple Disabilities, Including Sensory Impairment
Mary Booker
ISBN 978 1 84905 235 1
eISBN 978 0 85700 478 9

Group Music Activities for Adults with Intellectual and Developmental Disabilities
Maria Ramey
ISBN 978 1 84985 763 5
eISBN 978 0 85700 434 5

Portrait Therapy
Resolving Self-Identity Disruption in Clients with Life-Threatening and Chronic Illnesses
Susan M. D. Carr
ISBN 978 1 78592 293 0
eISBN 978 1 78450 605 6

Arts Therapists in Multidisciplinary Settings
Working Together for Better Outcomes
Edited by Caroline Miller
ISBN 978 1 84905 611 3
eISBN 978 1 78450 075 7

Assessment and Outcomes in the Arts Therapies
A Person-Centred Approach
Edited by Caroline Miller
ISBN 978 1 84905 414 0
eISBN 978 0 85700 788 9

ARTS THERAPIES WITH PEOPLE WITH PHYSICAL DISABILITIES

An Archetypal Approach

MARION GORDON-FLOWER

Foreword by Caroline Miller

Jessica Kingsley *Publishers*
London and Philadelphia

First published in 2020
by Jessica Kingsley Publishers
73 Collier Street
London N1 9BE, UK
and
400 Market Street, Suite 400
Philadelphia, PA 19106, USA

www.jkp.com

Copyright © Marion Gordon-Flower 2020
Foreword copyright © Caroline Miller 2020

Front cover image by the author: "Domains of Papatūānuku: earth, water, air, fire"

All rights reserved. No part of this publication may be reproduced in any material form (including photocopying, storing in any medium by electronic means or transmitting) without the written permission of the copyright owner except in accordance with the provisions of the law or under terms of a licence issued in the UK by the Copyright Licensing Agency Ltd. www.cla.co.uk or in overseas territories by the relevant reproduction rights organisation, for details see www.ifrro.org. Applications for the copyright owner's written permission to reproduce any part of this publication should be addressed to the publisher.

Warning: The doing of an unauthorised act in relation to a copyright work may result in both a civil claim for damages and criminal prosecution.

Library of Congress Cataloging in Publication Data
A CIP catalog record for this book is available from the Library of Congress

British Library Cataloguing in Publication Data
A CIP catalogue record for this book is available from the British Library

ISBN 978 1 78592 364 7
eISBN 978 1 78450 707 7

Printed and bound in the United States

Contents

Foreword by Caroline Miller 9

Acknowledgements 12

1. Overview and Introduction 13
   Overview 13
   Introduction 15

2. Developing Therapeutic Goal Plans 22
   Arts Therapy 5-Pt Star Model and assessment 22
   Goal setting with symbols and Arts Therapy 5-Pt Star combined . . 26
   Case study: Andy's goal setting using 5-Pt Star and symbols . . . 27
   Conclusion 31

3. Individual Arts Therapy 32
   Case study: Social story board 32
   Case study: Fairy Garden 40
   Summary and conclusion 48

4. Art Groups 49
   Case study: Ancient civilisations 50
   Case study: Goddess dolls 59
   Case study: Sacred vessels 68
   Conclusion 76

5. Environmental Sculpture 78
   The benefits and scope of using environmental media 79
   The Intervention in Nature process 80
   Case study: Jack's multimedia environmental sculpture process . . 83
   Time-Life-Lines 85

	Case study: Group journey through Time-Life-Lines.	86
	Introduction of the labyrinth for diverse contexts: trauma	90
	Conclusion.	93
6.	Expressive Dance Movement.	94
	Development of dance arts in a multidisciplinary team context . . .	94
	Case study: Legends of Maui.	98
	Case study: Around the World Through the Seasons	105
	Conclusion.	115
7.	Drama	116
	Introduction of dramatherapy within the context.	116
	Case study: Drama of *The King-Knight's Daughter*.	118
	Case study: Drama of *The International Convention of the Pacific* . .	124
	Conclusion.	131
8.	Music	132
	The arrival of music as a primary modality	132
	Music in multimodal arts therapy groups	135
	Case study: Voices of the Māori gods	137
	Case study: Yellow Bird.	141
	Conclusion.	143
9.	Models of Supervision within the Multidisciplinary Team .	144
	Seven-foci snapshots in symbols	145
	Conflict resolution using four elements	151
	Conclusion.	158
10.	Conclusion	159
	References.	161
	Further Reading	166
	Index	167

Figures

Figure 2.1 Arts Therapy 5-Pt Star Model in English and Māori.	23
Figure 2.2 Arts Therapy 5-Pt Star domains	23
Figure 2.3 Symbols suitable for people with hand impairments to hold	26
Figure 2.4 The participant (Andy) using a wheelchair tray for layout and reflection on symbols.	28
Figure 2.5 The dance arts group participant's (Andy's) symbols laid out in 5-Pt Star format.	29
Figure 3.1 Example of a relationship map using name tags and symbols	36
Figure 3.2 A similar smaller-sized tribute being released into water	38
Figure 3.3 Completed fairy garden.	43
Figure 3.4 Fairies in their garden.	44
Figure 3.5 Series of paintings "fairies in their garden".	45
Figure 3.6 Vision board cover.	47
Figure 3.7 Vision board internal	47
Figure 4.1 Research into symbols from ancient civilisations	51
Figure 4.2 Art by group members in responses to collages and hieroglyphics of name.	51
Figure 4.3 Mixed-media products used to transform plastic items into artefacts.	52
Figure 4.4 Ceremonial victory ladle for the gladiators of Rome with treasure box.	53
Figure 4.5 Vessel to hold gold coins for a prince, and a treasure box with treasures displayed.	55
Figure 4.6 Dual-purpose bowl of a chief for eating hangi and keeping his pet snake.	56
Figure 4.7 Inside the treasure box was the photo of a chief navigating the seas.	56
Figure 4.8 Museum poster to accompany the artefact exhibits when displayed.	57
Figure 4.9 Goddesses Maia and Cinderella	66
Figure 4.10 Artist A's testing of shape and media in collage	71
Figure 4.11 Artist A's sacred vessel marquette.	71
Figure 4.12 Artist B's testing of shape and media in collage	73
Figure 4.13 Artist B's sacred vessel marquette.	73
Figure 4.14 Artist C's sacred vessel marquette	75
Figure 5.1 Pairs sculpture using adjoined spiral shapes	81
Figure 5.2 Sculpture within features of environment, and painting from photograph.	81
Figure 5.3 Timeline chronology and nature objects; paintings of selected events.	88
Figure 5.4 Tributary monuments which integrated nature objects from timeline.	89
Figure 5.5 "Colours of my life and the sea" including more than 20 birthday celebrations	89
Figure 6.1 Dance 1 floor plan.	108
Figure 6.2 Dance 2 floor plan.	109
Figure 6.3 Dance 3 floor plan.	109
Figure 6.4 Dance 4 floor plan.	110
Figure 6.5 Dance 5 floor plan.	111

Figure 6.6 Dance 6 floor plan. 111
Figure 6.7 Dance 7 floor plan. 112
Figure 6.8 Dance 8 floor plan. 113
Figure 6.9 Embodying the role in dance 6. 114
Figure 6.10 Arriving home to *Aotearoa* (New Zealand) and "queenly power" in the final dance. 114
Figure 7.1 King Tupou, the Father-King from Samoa and Tonga; wants the best for his people and all people; costuming: Tongan cloth. 126
Figure 7.2 John Cruise, the Thief-Hero from California; Hollywood star—has stolen money to give to the poor of Africa; costuming: red, black, brown . . . 126
Figure 7.3 Sultan, the Hedonist-Lover from Arabia; travels with "a couple of birds"; holds "parties"; costuming: blue. 126
Figure 7.4 Count Ironstein, Engineer-Vampire from Madagascar; keeps people captive in a factory; costuming: orange. 126
Figure 7.5 Judge Bolyn, the Liberator-Judge from Sydney, Australia; uses a plane to rescue people; costuming: red 126
Figure 7.6 Night Warrior Zorro, the Knight-Shapeshifter from Auckland, New Zealand; travels undetected at night wearing a mask; costuming: blue 127
Figure 7.7 Santino, the Samaritan-Rescuer from Argentina; a cowboy who uses a lasso and gun; costuming: red, black, white 127
Figure 7.8 Akiiki, the Visionary-Priest from Uganda; performs the "opening blessing" for the conference; costuming: black tunic 127
Figure 7.9 Chef Wong, the Nature Lover from China; traveling chef who cooks amazing food; costuming: white shirt and chef's hat 127
Figure 7.10 The actors in their public performance at InterACT Festival in Auckland. 130
Figure 8.1 Singing on stage at InterACT Festival 134
Figure 9.1 Holding the four archetypal elements 152

Tables

Table 2.1 Andy's 5-Pt Star goal symbols 29
Table 4.1 Historical use of dolls. 60
Table 4.2 Step 1: Format questionnaire 64
Table 4.3 Step 2: Changing the skin tone, eye colour and hairstyle 65
Table 4.4 Step 3: Goddess clothing and special equipment 66
Table 6.1 Personal history of participants relevant to roles (group 1) 101
Table 6.2 Personal history of participants relevant to roles (group 2) 103
Table 6.3 Participants' choices of seasons, songs and localities 107
Table 7.1 Comparison between roles in the two dramas. 125
Table 8.1 Participants' musical abilities and interests. 138
Table 8.2 Participants' roles and instrument choices 140
Table 9.1 Traits and attributes of the four elements. 153

Foreword

This book is the account of work with a group of people in a particular setting. The work takes place within the health and disability sector in NGOs. The participants are adults with physical and other disabilities, which require most of them to have full-time residential care. Most of these people have multiple disabilities. Their support staff include residential care staff, occupational therapists, physiotherapists, nurses and one arts therapist. Marion, the arts therapist, has her own approach which sees disabilities not as handicaps or exclusionary factors, but as genuine challenges requiring support staff to take a problem-solving approach to enable access to a range of activities open to their non-disabled peers.

Marion's approach uses multimodal arts therapies and an ecological view of the client group which includes all aspects of each person and their lives, including life experience, ethnicity, current living environment, needs and desires, and spiritual experiences and beliefs. Her focus is always on how each person can live the fullest life possible.

These adults are mostly in residential care, with many dependent on staff for most of their physical needs. They face challenges of moderate to severe physical and communication difficulties. Disabilities include severe physical impairments, coordination difficulties, non-verbal or verbal difficulties, hearing and sight impairments, cognitive difficulties, autism and epilepsy. Arts therapies are available to the residents and privately funded clients on an individual or group basis. The approach allows a fluid connection between ideas, artwork, movement, research projects, music and drama. There is a focus on embodiment through the arts, encouraging a fuller connection to, and expression of, each person's full range of experience and emotion. Importance is placed on how people can communicate about their lives, the things that matter to them and the goals they have for themselves. This encompasses romantic longings for relationship, obtaining paid work, being recognised as artists, increasing social experiences, having exhibitions at which their work sells, attending family events and funerals, and building family contacts where appropriate.

Marion's approach represents social justice in action, although she does not approach this as a mission or attempt to persuade others to adopt that philosophy. She is very persuasive within institutions and workplaces, seeing beyond basic needs for shelter, food and other physical needs being met. She extended her role to include finding organisations to provide part-time or short-term work for some of the adults who wanted to work with the police, in special schools or elsewhere in the community. She also managed to obtain special funding to cover transport to the workplace and the support of an assistant if required. As part of her work she developed a community-liaison role. She did this without pretension or preaching but rather in a practical and matter-of-fact manner.

Working with symbols and archetypes is at the heart of her approach. This takes the person to a level of abstraction, imagination and learning which immediately lifts and deepens the possibilities of a range of responses. She becomes a fellow traveller, on a spiritual journey, providing resources for the journey based on the level of interest shown in the range of possibilities she offers.

Marion provides a rich selection of resources, which include research via the Internet or stories, the stimulation of symbols and archetypal cards, colours, fabrics and musical instruments. All of these can prompt and stimulate imaginative and emotional responses. She provides a richness of resources and stimulation to initiate ideas, and then continues to feed and nourish them to full development.

This approach using archetypes and symbols, and with the provision of rich resources, works well with this client group, but it would be equally applicable to other client groups because of its ability to stimulate imagination beyond the practicalities or difficulties of everyday life.

The benefits were seen in individual work, and perhaps even more evidently in groupwork. In the groups social interactions and cohesion added another level of therapeutic benefit in joint projects and performances. The responses to archetypal figures, symbols and stories opened social connection and possibilities in fun and engaging ways. In addition, the people involved learned techniques and processes while participating; they engaged with people of different ethnicities and backgrounds, and found common purpose and ground. The participants also engaged in self-assessment to increase their self-awareness of achievement and self-respect.

Marion's work demonstrates the power of the arts therapies to move participants beyond everyday limitations and concerns into realms and roles and relationships previously not experienced. This opens the possibility of future, further expansion in each person's life.

Caroline Miller
Drama Therapist, Clinical Psychologist and Supervisor in Private Practice
MNZAC, Member of New Zealand Association of Counsellors
BADTh, International Member of The British Association of Drama Therapists

Acknowledgements

A big thank you to everyone who contributed to this project, too numerous to name. This work happened within a vibrant and creative community, which included people with disabilities, family members, support staff, team members and managers. The focus was on how we could live our best lives together and I am so grateful for the journeys that we made.

Special thanks to Caroline Miller, who has influenced my path as a practitioner through the course of my Masters degree and as my long-term clinical supervisor; and also in encouraging and editing my writing. Her skills and support have been a light and an anchor in the navigation of this work. My gratitude to her is beyond measure. Also, to Jean Parkinson for supervision using Sandplay and during the creation of the initial Arts Therapy 5-Pt Star concept; and who gifted the archetypal cards which are featured in this book.

Kia ora to Anaru Te Tai and Tipene Lemon for support and advice in tikanga Māori and translation in te reo.

Special thanks to Lynette, Libby, Shannon, Patricia, Paul, Jimmy, Marilyn, Steph, Oliver, Augi, Michael, Visi, Yung, Yuri and John, all of whom made significant contributions to the project in different ways.

Thank you to my husband, Rod Flower, who is a loyal companion and inspiration within our shared professional interests and life together. Also, to our family who are generous with their love and support.

Kia ora koutou. "Naku te rourou, nau te rourou, ka ora ai te iwi." With your basket and my basket, the people will be nourished.

CHAPTER 1

Overview and Introduction

Keywords: physical disabilities, multicultural, multidisciplinary, archetypal scope, psychosocial factors

Overview

This book offers a series of case studies about work which took place through individual and group multimodal arts therapy within a health and disability organisation in Auckland, New Zealand (*Aotearoa* in Māori), a bicultural Pacific nation of European and Māori people with diverse immigrant populations. Multimodal arts therapy was provided through a rehabilitation service alongside physiotherapy and occupational therapy, within a larger multidisciplinary team that provided services in residential, daily-living and community support.

Although the case studies took place with people who had physical disabilities as a primary diagnosis, the use of archetypal approaches and their power to engage dynamic transformational processes could equally be applied in other contexts. The client group presented with a range of significant disability challenges including the following:

- Being confined to a wheelchair
- Upper-limb contractions/hand impairments
- Coordination difficulties
- Dysarthria, being "non-verbal" or cognitive difficulties affecting verbal communication
- Being blind and autistic

Additionally, there were medical conditions which required collaborative care within the arts therapy sessions which included:

- Epilepsy
- Peg feeding
- Tractotomy

Within the wider multidisciplinary team, physical needs were the primary focus of most staff, who were nurses, support workers, a physiotherapist and physio-assistant, and often took priority for the occupational therapist who was responsible for the acquisition of mobility equipment and for modifying environments toward accessibility. The arts therapist offered a key avenue to explore wellbeing in a holistic way whereby psychological, emotional, spiritual and social needs could take a greater point of focus. This assisted in the formulation of goal plans that were based on self-awareness and knowledge, rather than in response to a health-services requirement. As the arts therapist role became established within the organisation, a new role of community connector was also introduced, which assisted with the accessing of resources that aligned with goal plans.

Multimodal arts therapy provided the opportunity for people who had significant physical mobility and communication challenges to work in their most accessible and preferred arts modes. It also offered intermodal avenues which reduced the need for verbal communication and, at the same time, extended the therapeutic benefits. Participants were able to articulate their personal preferences, cultural identity and aspirations in ways that could be understood by others, which led to more fulfilling lives.

Due to the role that arts therapy took in the maintenance of wellbeing, many of the participants attended long term. This led to the exploration of a diverse range of processes in response to their personal growth and unfolding needs, which effectively continued the therapeutic dynamic. Archetypal approaches were discovered to be effective within the explored modalities of art, environmental sculpture, drama, expressive dance movement and music. Archetypal approaches were also incorporated within supervision for interns and volunteers, who assisted in the arts therapy service to gain practical experience.

It is hoped that the arts therapy interventions and supervision approaches provided here will be adaptable for arts therapists and allied professionals working in different contexts. At the same time, the first intention in writing this book has been to address the gap in literature available to practitioners who work with people who have physical disabilities.

Introduction
Practise-based inquiry
As a multimodal arts therapist working in the health field with a client group who had physical disabilities, there was an informal line of inquiry which took place daily. The question posed was, "Given the physical barriers to full and free participation, what are the most effective approaches to engage this client or this group in therapy?" This question helped to shape the course of person-centred individualised arts therapy, group therapy and the way in which the service evolved over a seven-year period. The day-by-day inquiry became a form of practise-based research as a pattern emerged through observations made across modalities over time. Eventually there was a moment of realisation that interventions that appeared to have the most therapeutic impact had a commonality that could possibly be termed "archetypal."

Understanding the term "archetypal"
A new question then presented of "What exactly is 'the archetype' and how can this best be shared with other therapists?" Of this, there has been something of an elusiveness in the quest for concise wording. Roesler (2012) points out that archetypes are problematic to define because "a huge number of things and very different concepts are called archetypal" (p.6).

The archetypal concepts used in arts therapy over the period touched on a range of different areas and explored some of the practical frameworks provided by Jungian psychologists which included the following:

- Symbolic objects (e.g. figurines, everyday objects used in a symbolic way)
- Symbolic shapes (e.g. egg, spiral, circle, cross)
- Mythological stories (e.g. legends of Maui, Persephone and the seasons)

- Creation of mythological characters (e.g. fairies, goddesses)
- Use of narrative patterns (e.g. kings and their kingdoms)
- Rituals (e.g. tributes, homecoming)
- Spiritual notions (e.g. biblical references, festivals of sacred celebration)

Although seemingly diverse, these concepts had the commonality of providing points of entry into the imaginal realm in ways that were engaging, energising and transformational. Carl Jung theorised that:

> …archetypes are inherited, inborn, structural dispositions with respect to the species-specific modes of behaviour of human beings…they express themselves in typical actions, similar in all human beings… [and] also have a form of expression that can only be perceived inwardly within the psyche, that is, in feelings, emotions, mythical fantasy images, and "mythical" primal ideas. (von Franz 1999, p.6)

In formulating his theories, Jung was said to have worked with multiple viewpoints. "As a scientist he presented his ideas in a clear and understandable way"; on the other hand, "it is almost as if he… [invited] different inner voices to speak" which could appear to be contradictory, leaving "the reader… in a state of questioning and wonder" (Chodorow 1997, p.3). It seemed fitting to arrive at a standpoint where the term "archetypal" was best unpacked and revealed through multiple perspectives. This offered the mirroring of how archetypal engagement arose through the unconscious to interplay with the conscious mind, through glimpses rather than the fully formed idea. As suggested by Roesler (2012), "the true archetype is not accessible for consciousness but is of a transcendental nature" (p.227).

Jung devised the notion that the conscious and unconscious mind were "in opposition" through which transformational processes arose (von Franz 1999, pp.9–11) and that the two also "interact as a part of a finely tuned equilibrium" (p.10). McNiff (2017) stated, "Like so many other people I found my way to the arts in therapy through experiences with artistic knowing and healing; the pattern is archetypal." He further stated that "art processes…[are] a number of steps ahead of knowing and the reflecting mind" (p.275). Scategni (2015) offered that "archetypal images…serve as a gateway between physical reality and the so-called 'reality of the soul'" (p.29). Knill (2017a) also described two different states: "the habitual experience of worlding as in everyday life" alongside of "things emerging from an imaginary space…[in an] 'other' or 'alternative' experience of worlding" (p.35). Each of these perspectives were helpful when considering the archetypal in action within a multimodal arts therapeutic space.

Multimodal arts therapy offered two or more modalities within groups and sometimes individual sessions, which provided multiple points of entry into the therapeutic processes and intermodal fluidity, whereby one creative process could be responded to with another. This maximised the opportunities for engagement from the perspective of deepening the process within the unconscious mind. Through this, different modality preferences were catered for and the creative variety offered greater stimulation. Participants could become multiskilled in arts therapy processes and in arts techniques, which facilitated their goals of participating in public forums to promote disability awareness and advocacy.

Applying the archetypal approach in a multicultural context

The nature and origins of archetypes have been the subject of long-term scientific debate. Jung (1964) stated that "Just as the human body represents a whole museum of organs, each with a long evolutionary history behind it, so we should expect to find that the mind is organized in a similar way" (p.67).

> Preformationism in biology is the view that the information for producing an organism is contained in the zygote and becomes "read-out" in an environment. The parallel position in analytical psychology is that archetypes are pre-existent in the psyche and are "read-out" into experience. (Merchant 2009, p.340)

Recent viewpoints have included that "archetypes [are] emergent structures resulting from a developmental interaction between genes and environment that is unique for each person" (Merchant 2009, p.342). With this in mind, in providing multimodal arts therapy for people from a wide range of ethnicities and backgrounds, there was a further question to address of whether archetypal interventions would prove equally as relevant across cultures. Observations in practice indicated that the archetypal modes used were equally accessible to all participants, who could relate them in ways specific to their own culture of origin and background.

von Franz (1999, p.44) suggested that there are four levels of the unconscious as follows:

- personal unconscious [repressed memories]
- group unconscious [e.g. *whanau*, families]
- unconsciousness of large-scale national unities [symbols specific to ethnicities]
- universal archetypal structures [common to all of humanity].

This appeared to explain how archetypes resonated with group participants who were of diverse backgrounds and could be personalised in ways that were relevant to their individual therapeutic needs.

Limitations in Jungian approaches applied

Jung developed an understanding of archetypal systems through his practice with psychiatric patients and other therapists who consulted with him. Through tapping into their unconscious processes, particularly their dream symbolism, he was able to facilitate their healing and personal growth through analysis. Jungian or analytical psychologists worked with analysis as a foundation of their practice.

It is important to clarify that analysis was outside the scope of practice in arts therapy. There have been references made to Jung's theories of anima and animus, individuation, and meanings attributed to symbols, which helped to inform the understanding of the therapist. However, at the time of therapy, meaning making remained predominantly with the client. This approach aligned with the perspectives expressed by Granot, Regev and Snir (2017):

> Since JT [Jungian Art Therapists] trusts clients' conscious and unconscious forces and their creative abilities, the therapist is perceived as someone who facilitates and accompanies a natural developmental process, both humbly and empathically: "It means relinquishing the superior place of the one who knows what's best for the clients. I really don't think I'm smarter than my clients. I'm together with them." (p.5)
>
> Interpretation is something that can kill a therapeutic process, since the psyche has its own way…we only see the tip of the iceberg. [It is preferable that] clients arrive at their own interpretation by themselves. (p.9)

Archetypal approaches as a therapeutic doorway

Where physical mobility and limited vocal abilities presented barriers, archetypal approaches provided opportunities for a form of liberation into unconscious creative processes. Leading researcher and practitioner in arts therapies, Rainbow Ho (Ho 2017), has been able to articulate her personal experience of becoming temporarily non-verbal in childhood. She has described complex thought processes that delayed her ability to take part in social conversation to the point of completely withdrawing from verbalising. She stated that, rather than being sent for psychiatric diagnosis and treatment as one might have expected, she was sent to dance, which "opened a door to a huge world" in which she found herself "totally free."

Although there are obvious differences, a parallel can be drawn with Ho's sense of liberation in dance movement. Many of the arts therapy participants were non-verbal through delay in thought processes caused by brain injury at birth or physical paralysis, or through deterioration in health which had affected speech later in life; however, they also experienced a level of physical entrapment that prevented them from finding the open door that Ho found through dance. On the other hand, openings appeared through the archetypal approach across the multiple modalities. Although the modalities provide a significant therapeutic dimension, the mind engagement toward archetypal aspects of the interventions and the embodiment of them were more notably transformational.

Arts therapy for disability within public health

Baum (2016) stated that people who have disabilities that used public health services experienced higher levels of poverty and lower levels in overall health, education outcomes and opportunities to create income. She pointed out that there can be challenges at every turn within daily living, where assistance is required to participate in each aspect of ordinary life, and has suggested that services remain inadequate (pp.273–274). Baum has stated that "isolation" and "poor social networks" are significant in terms of "psychosocial risk factors," which result in "poor health." Lack of true citizenship and personal power, and "low self-esteem" were also factors (p.325).

She further stated that "long-term chronic stress" resulted in "chronic disease, depression and anxiety" (p.331). Of the stressors named, the following can be identified as directly impacting the client group:

- Lack of control over…home life
- Poverty—managing on a low income
- Discrimination
- Social isolation and lack of meaningful contacts
- Unemployment
- Barriers to seeking mental health care: cultural, financial, class, gender

(Baum 2016)

Additional factors have been identified as follows:

- Birth and childhood trauma through medical interventions and institutionalisation
- Attachment and abandonment issues
- Lack of recognised personal and cultural identity
- Physical and emotional abuse

Archetypal approaches were particularly effective in meeting the needs for recovery from deep psychological wounding, in ways that were containable within group forums. Privacy, confidentiality and anonymity were difficult to preserve because people often attended groups with their flatmates or support staff, who would have been able to misuse sensitive material if this was disclosed. Working on a symbolic level through archetypal approaches provided emotional safety and therapeutic integration. Importantly, the service users involved found it enjoyable and were able to be playful in the process.

Comparison of disability context with other client groups

Howie, Prasad and Kristel (2013) provided a variety of studies related to diverse populations and cultural groups, which offered useful parallels. Glassman (2013) described a school cohort where skill development was a part of an art studio approach and an exhibition was a part of the therapy contract (pp.153–181). The client group with disabilities held similar therapeutic contracts and goals. Councill and Phlegar (2013) explored what it meant to live with a diagnosis of being medically fragile and with a reduced life expectancy, and how art therapy contributed to their wellbeing (pp.203–213). Medical vulnerability, age-related physical deterioration and shortened life expectancy affected most of the rehabilitation-service participants.

On the other hand, disparities in relationship to people with disabilities were also identified. Sobol and Howie (2013) described the influence of generational family patterns which impacted childhood development and the establishment of "cultural norms" (pp.245–255). This led to the question of what might have happened in the absence of the recognised family influences, as a significant number of service users were separated from their birth family and institutionalised in infancy. Their upbringing had a pathway that had led to the membership of a form of marginalised subculture. Furthermore, Gnatt (2013) offered the perspective that response to trauma was universal while interpretation of the experience had culturally based components evident through art interventions (pp.234–244). When considering the "*Instinctual Trauma Response*" (p.236; original italics), it is important to acknowledge that there was no "fight-or-flight" option for people who were unable to mobilise independently, and to appreciate on an empathetic level how this might amplify and intensify traumatic experiences.

The collaborative journey

Arts therapy provided a means of expressing and dealing with challenges that people with physical disabilities faced that were common to humanity, and those that went beyond the day-to-day struggles experienced by people who are "fully able-bodied." The needs, interests, creativity, abilities and courage of this client group led the way at each stage. As their arts therapist, I was privileged to be their agent of archetypal modes, witness to their progress and companion on their creative therapeutic journeys, which they were eager to share for the benefit of others globally.

CHAPTER 2

Developing Therapeutic Goal Plans

Keywords: Arts Therapy 5-Pt Star Model, symbols, archetypal cards, visual goal setting, self-evaluation

Arts Therapy 5-Pt Star Model and assessment

The Arts Therapy 5-Pt Star Model was initially created as a poster diagram in 2008 (Gordon-Flower 2014a, p.51) in English and later translated into Māori to promote a shared understanding of therapeutic focus and potential areas of benefit for multimodal arts therapy groups within a community context of self-referring adults. The poster was viewed and discussed at the beginning of sessions with the understanding that each of five domains would be included, which provided a balanced approach. The five domains were self-reflection, transformational engagement/action, relationships, aesthetic skills/process and lifestyle development (Figures 2.1 and 2.2 show recent versions of the model created for use in different group settings). The question posed at the end of each session was, "What will you take away from the therapeutic space that can help you in your life?"

The model was adopted within the health and disability organisation in 2009, and the five domains were developed into Arts Therapy 5-Pt Star Assessment, an outcomes tool which was refined in practice (Gordon-Flower 2014a, b, 2016). The Arts Therapy 5-Pt Star Assessment documented outcomes alongside of those provided by physiotherapy and occupational therapy within the rehabilitation context. The model and assessment were holistic and compatible with strength-based models that had been adopted within the health and disability sector in *Aotearoa* (New Zealand), including Charles Rapp Strengths Model, Person Centred Plan (PCP) and *Te Whare Tapa Whā* Māori Model of Health. The method of assessment was based on a combination of arts therapist observations and feedback from the client and/or significant others (i.e. family and support staff).

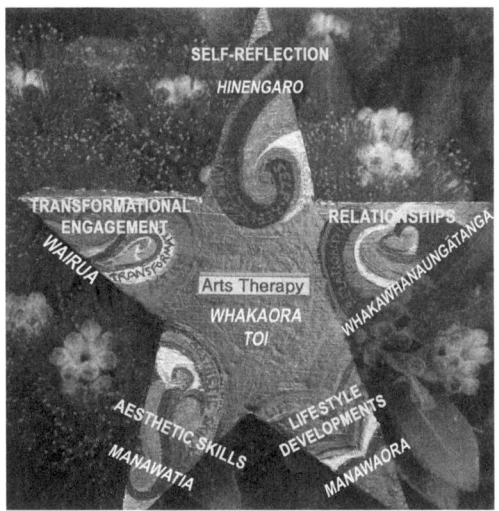

Figure 2.1 Arts Therapy 5-Pt Star Model in English and Māori (see insert for colour version)

Figure 2.2 Arts Therapy 5-Pt Star domains (see insert for colour version)

In 2012, the assessment tool became the subject of an international research study through New Zealand Health and Disability Commission (H&DC) Northern X Ethics Committee to establish the applicability of the five domains and assessment methods to arts therapists and their client groups in other contexts (Gordon-Flower 2016, pp.70–71). The results demonstrated applicability of the five domains and adaptability of the assessment for different contexts on an individual basis.

One of the outcomes of the study was the development of a self-evaluation form that was useful for people who have a range of different kinds of abilities and disabilities, to evaluate and share their own progress. This was designed to be accessible to people who had profound mobility disabilities and were non-verbal, as well as those who were verbally articulate and more highly functioning physically. Strategies included an interview approach, the use of large font size for participants who had sight impairments, and choices through tick lists and rating scales. There were also open questions. For those who were non-verbal, the therapist provided possibilities for their selection, relying on her knowledge of the person from various therapeutic encounters. The combined approaches proved an effective means for participants to give feedback about their own progress, and helped to develop individual and group therapeutic goals at the next stage.

Both the assessment tool and the self-evaluation form were accepted by government funding agencies as a valid means of providing relevant qualitative and quantitative data in reporting. Both methods were instrumental in ensuring that the arts therapy opportunities remained available for people with disabilities through the rehabilitation service. Ultimately, the option of service users being able to give direct feedback through the self-evaluation form on the benefits and challenges of participating in the arts therapies was recognised as preferable to being assessed by others.

Use of symbols in individual and group therapy
In addition to the more formalised approaches to goal setting and progress reporting, arts-based approaches were utilised to establish goals and reflect upon outcomes. Symbols were particularly effective as these were frequently used for individual art therapy and multimodal groups, and this medium could easily be adopted toward goals and outcomes.

In the use of symbols in therapy there was some alignment with Sandplay therapy. Friedman and Mitchelle (2008) stated, "Sandplay… creates a concrete manifestation of…[the client's] imaginal world… illuminates [their] symbolic world and provides a safe container, the sandtray" (p.1). In Sandplay therapy, miniature figurines are used to create what often emerges to be a layered three-dimensional picture in sand. The client may mould the sand into undulations and shapes, bury some objects while elevating others and could pour water into the tray, all of which is significant to the therapeutic process (Granot *et al.* 2017, p.6). This would not have been physically possible for most of the clients in the service.

Symbols provided an accessible doorway into the imaginal realm and transformational processes without the need for analysis, whereby the therapist was a witness to the participant's process and "midwife [to a form of] birthing process" (Granot *et al.* 2017, p.9). Intermodal approaches were used to extend and deepen the therapeutic encounter and create a dialogue between externalised creative expressions in different modalities (McNiff 1992, 2004; Knill, Levine and Levine 2005; Levine and Levine 2017). In the rehabilitation context where many arts therapy participants had dysarthria or were non-verbal, dialoguing took place through modes that did not require speech.

There were practical considerations in providing symbols for use in the rehabilitation setting, in that they needed to be visually and physically accessible for use in both individual therapy and groups, for clients who were dependent upon physical assistance to participate. They needed to be large enough to be seen for selection by those who had partial vision, and suitable to hold by those with coordination difficulties and hand impairments; and easily retrieved by the therapist and assistants if dropped into wheelchairs or onto the floor. Being able to claim and physically hold symbols of significance was an important aspect of therapeutic engagement and process. Wheelchair trays could be effectively utilised to provide a form of containment similar to that of sand trays and also provided the required visual and physical accessibility. Alternatively, a sheet of art paper was laid on a table as a means of providing containment.

In group contexts of dance arts and drama, symbols were frequently chosen to support character roles and carried into the movement or dramatic space. The symbols shown in Figure 2.3 were of a suitable size for participants to hold, or to have placed on their lap or alongside them in their wheelchairs. Smaller objects chosen had rings attached which could be looped over a finger and successfully held.

Figure 2.3 Symbols suitable for people with hand impairments to hold

Ways of using symbols for goals and outcomes

Participants were asked to do the following:

- Choose two symbols or groups of symbols in response to the statement, "Where I have arrived at now, and where I want to be."
- Choose symbols for "The greatest highlight of the arts therapy journey made, and what I hope to achieve in my life in the coming year."

Goal setting with symbols and Arts Therapy 5-Pt Star combined

At the beginning of a new group process in dance arts, the first three sessions were focused on establishing personal and group goals.

Session 1

Each person selected two archetypal cards from 74 different possibilities (Myss 2003) to create a character role that they wanted to explore through weekly dance sessions and which held character strengths on which they wished to focus in their day-to-day lives. The cards were enlarged on a colour photocopier for greater visibility and so that they could be utilised by the participants throughout the year.

Session 2
Each person chose a song that would facilitate the expression of the character through the dance. The group began to consider possibilities for a theme that could unite their archetypal roles and diverse music choices in choreography and performance.

Session 3
The Arts Therapy 5-Pt Star was presented in large format. Words were chosen to describe each of the five domains as they applied to the intermodal dance, providing terms that the participants would most readily understand (see Figure 2.5):

- Self-reflection: tuning in with myself; how I feel/think
- Growth-change process: being involved in doing
- Relationships: enjoying getting on with others
- Learning and growing: more arts/dance skills
- Lifestyle and confidence: taking my archetype with me into life

Participants chose objects for each of the five domains to symbolise how they would like this aspect of their lives to develop or be maintained. This helped them to make stronger connections between the modalities and the potential therapeutic benefits through the 5-Pt Star framework.

Case study: Andy's goal setting using 5-Pt Star and symbols

Andy was a man in his 50s who had dysarthria, and for whom verbal communication was very challenging. He had good upper-limb movement with minimal impairment to his hands and good coordination. He used a hand-operated motorised wheelchair for mobility. He was able to pull himself up by using a bar at the gym and then stand for limited periods. He attended both dance arts and drama groups and had a triumphant moment on stage in a dance performance in which he and a stage partner succeeded in pulling themselves up out of their wheelchairs and stood unexpectedly for the audience. This had taken many weeks of hard work at the gym, in preparation, and practice in leading the group choreography in dance arts group.

In his 5-Pt Star Evaluation form interviews, Andy indicated a preference for drama. Participating in dance arts choreography could be challenging in terms of keeping up with group movements in his motorised wheelchair. He greatly enjoyed creating and embodying character roles in both groups and being involved in creating costumes. He was able to paint independently from a paint tray with a brush once these were set up and his paper fixed to the table, an aspect of the intermodal arts therapy that he also enjoyed. In symbol work, he was always ready to select objects when they were laid out on a low-level table, a process which would help him to externalise his thoughts and feelings. He was able to pick up, hold and position the selected symbols once they were placed on his wheelchair tray (Figure 2.4).

Figure 2.4 The participant (Andy) using a wheelchair tray for layout and reflection on symbols (see insert for colour version)

In approaching the 5-Pt Star format in dance arts, Andy had chosen "virgin" and "mystic" cards (Myss 2003) as a focus for character development, which became central in the chart layout for his goal planning. He had chosen the song "It Must Have Been Love" by Roxette to support his character role and contribute to the group dance. In the combination of the cards and the song that he had chosen, there was the suggestion that he was moving on from a romantic-relationship attachment and claiming a new start with a focus toward his spiritual qualities and strengths. Figure 2.5 shows Andy's symbols laid out in 5-Pt Star format.

DEVELOPING THERAPEUTIC GOAL PLANS 29

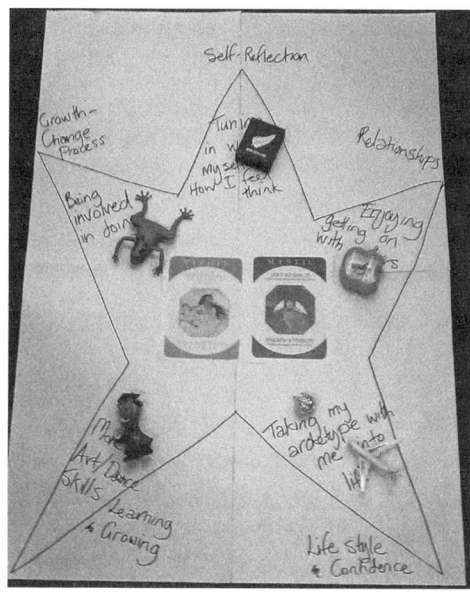

Figure 2.5 The dance arts group participant's (Andy's) symbols laid out in 5-Pt Star format (see insert for colour version)

Andy's choices of symbolic objects were a mixture of personal, cultural and archetypal, and fitted into the 5-Pt Star format (Table 2.1).

Table 2.1 Andy's 5-Pt Star goal symbols

5-Pt Star domain	Statement on chart	Andy's choices
Self-reflection	Tuning in with myself; how I think/feel	Solid black box with the silver-fern emblem and "New Zealand" in text used by "the All Blacks Rugby team." Recognised as a symbol of masculinity and national identity.
Transformational engagement/action	Growth-change process; being involved in doing	A frog, archetypal symbol of transformation, and a reptilian animal that can swim well in water and move in leaps and bounds on lily pads and dry land.
Relationships	Enjoying getting on with others	A pink clock in the shape of an apple with a bite taken out of it. The object was playful and suggested indulgence. It also suggested the passing of time, the need to be proactive with plans, and that things can take place at the right time through synchronicity.

cont.

5-Pt Star domain	Statement on chart	Andy's choices
Aesthetic skills/ process	Learning and growing	A bear wearing an academic gown and cap, holding a book indicating learning which has outcomes and rewards.
Lifestyle development	Taking my archetype with me into life	Two objects selected: a mirrored multifaceted ball as used over disco dance floors, and an aeroplane. There was the sense of someone who wanted to go out and have fun and be dynamic in his relationships and approach to life.

Although I made the above observations, I took the role of witness alongside the group members. I wanted to avoid any interjection of meaning that might confuse his own meaning making. Once the objects had been correctly positioned on the chart and he was fully satisfied with it, I went through each of the 5-Pt Star domains, reading out the statement as written on the chart and making an acknowledgement of his chosen objects. My comments were factually based, minimal and questioning: "Kiwi and All Blacks symbol?" "A frog that can take leaps?" "That looks like a fun kind of clock?" "That is a bear who is graduating?" "A disco ball and a plane together? That looks like fun to be had too!" In each case, Andy had confirmed that my observations were on the right track as we spent time appreciating his goals layout as a witnessing group.

Some months later, there were key indicators that Andy had made changes aligned with the goals he had set using the symbols and 5-pt Star chart combination. The next significant song choice he made for choreography in dance arts was "Hot, Hot, Hot" by Vengaboys. This begins, "I've got fire in my pants!" The YouTube video which we downloaded as a backdrop showed beach party scenes, people having fun and dancing in a sexually provocative manner. It was almost the opposite of the slow, nostalgic, slightly sad rendition of "It Must Have Been Love" by Roxette that had accompanied his archetypal cards of "virgin" and "mystic" in the previous dance process. Andy had arrived, at least in an emotional sense, at the place that he had visualised through the use of symbols in the lifestyle domain of the 5-Pt Star format shown in Figure 2.5. He was no longer inviting the group to join him in a reflective space of reminiscence and letting go, but rather to experience being in the moment, exploring the vitality and vibrancy of his chosen song and the accompanying dance movements. He had arrived at a place of being fully present and free of the past, ready to engage in the spontaneous and sensual. The dance arts group were able to support this new stage of his journey by drawing upon some of the choreography in the Vengaboys' video, which they performed at their next stage show, with the majority being in wheelchairs.

Conclusion

The most recent development in the Arts Therapy 5-Pt Star Model and Assessment has been the introduction of a self-evaluation process through which clients with disabilities, including those who were non-verbal, were able to provide feedback as a basis for therapeutic goal plans. It was also possible for the client group to utilise the Arts Therapy 5-Pt Star format with symbols to set their own therapeutic goals and to draw upon the archetypal approach.

Symbols provided a means of self-reflection, and the arts therapeutic process proved to be immediately engaging and accessible to the participants who had physical disabilities. When combined with the Arts Therapy 5-Pt Star format, participants were readily able to set therapeutic goals appropriate to the modalities used, which had personal significance and meaning, and engaged the unconscious mind. Andy's goal setting and therapeutic engagement brought about progress related to his chosen symbols. The therapeutic journey that he made based on his symbolic goal setting led him into a new phase of emotional wellbeing where he had a greater capacity to be present.

CHAPTER 3

Individual Arts Therapy

Keywords: trauma, symbols, fairies, ritual, homecoming, individuation, animus, twins

Two individual art therapy case studies are presented which demonstrate how person-centred approaches can lead to very different therapeutic journeys which align with clients' therapeutic goals and their individualised ways of participating. In the case of Maia, a social story board was used which was laid out in symbols. A second archetypal approach emerged of a tribute and ritual ceremony, which was an appropriate way of bringing closure and integration. In the case of Jamie, a goal of creating a fairy garden as a living artwork arose through a process. Alongside the primary focus of creating the fairies and their garden, a self-directed painting process took place. The paintings revealed that through engagement in the archetype of fairies there were suggestions of individuation. Both women took a path that was highly engaged with the archetype, which was transformational for them.

Case study: Social story board
Client background
Maia was a woman in her late 30s who had cerebral palsy which significantly affected her mobility and speech. She was unable to walk and had contracted upper limbs and hands. She used a head-driven motorised wheelchair for mobility and painted using a paintbrush taped to a head wand. She also had dysarthria and used her head wand with a communication device or spell chart to verbally articulate. She was

referred to arts therapy by a psychologist from a dual disability mental health team. He was assisting her to develop emotion modulation strategies and recognised that arts therapy could help her to explore unresolved grief.

Arts therapy overview

Arts therapy took place weekly through six 1-hour sessions using the following approaches:

1. Developing a relationship map and social story board using symbols

2. Creating a tribute and holding a ritual ceremony

3. Painting on canvas

4. Sharing the journey with her mentor

Due to the sensitive nature of the traumatic events that unfolded, Maia provided parameters for sharing her story. She stated that I could share the process that we developed together in the sessions, but not the content of her personal experience; also, that I could reconstruct visual scenarios similar to those used, but could not use the photographs of her own work. (Maia has heard the case study read aloud and has given her full approval for this to be published.)

History through arts therapy programme

When Maia first attended one-to-one sessions seven years earlier she was 30 years old and it seemed as if her whole identity was consumed by past trauma (Lubin and Johnson 2008, pp.64–65), the most poignant being separation from her birth mother in early childhood. McAdams (1993) stated, "The first two years of life leave us with a set of unconscious and nonverbal 'attitudes' about self, and world, and about how the three relate to each other" (p.47). The difficulties posed by her disability impacted her primary relationship in a way that led to her institutionalisation. Through the course of her life she had also encountered physical, emotional and sexual abuse, which resulted in complex symptoms of post-traumatic stress disorder (Lubin and Johnson 2008; Rothschild 2000). Although seemingly encapsulated in trauma and grief, and also living with overwhelming disability challenges, Maia demonstrated exceptional intellectual abilities and a strong desire to establish a meaningful adult life.

Over the seven years, Maia had concurrently attended both individual arts therapy sessions for depth therapy and multimodal arts therapy groups to work with themes of identity, self-esteem, relationships and confidence building. She also attended personal development groups to explore vocational interests, where she created a video showing herself performing five key abilities aligned with her aspirations of working with children. At 33 years old, she became a volunteer teacher aide who inspired and motivated children with disabilities in learning to use equipment that she had struggled with herself and then mastered. The focus of Maia's individual arts therapy sessions then shifted onto the task of maintaining her volunteer job role, and also creating a self-published book about moving beyond her disability.

At 36 years old, Maia had encountered a setback when her efforts to reconnect with her birth family became thwarted, resulting in a mental health crisis. She was being treated by a clinical psychologist who sought my collaboration to provide her history and establish complementary treatment plans. After a period of treatment, he had asked if I could assist her to explore an area of grief that he thought she was "stuck on," so that their sessions could remain focused on developing emotion-modulation strategies.

Overview of interventions and outcomes

At the point of referral, Maia's "stuckness in grief" was identified as relating to a significant person who had died a few years before. The idea of creating a modified social atom came to mind, as this would be a client-led process and there would be an invitation for the area of "stuckness" to emerge in a phenomenological way. If the loss of the person arose in the process as expected, she could potentially draw strength from the bigger picture of her life in relationships. However, the process revealed that Maia was not actually grieving for the loss of the person, but rather angry about their handling of a situation which had compounded the pain of unresolved traumatic events.

Throughout the sessions, Maia was able to fully disclose events which had taken place 15 years prior. Throughout the archetypal arts therapy processes of symbols and rituals, the pieces of a jigsaw puzzle fitted back together in her memories and she was able to arrive at a point of resolution. She has since been able to move beyond the trauma and claim the next stage of her life.

Arts therapy sessions
Sessions 1 and 2: Developing a relationships map and social story board using symbols

We began by joining four A2-size sheets of paper together to create a large area on which to map out Maia's relationships by using name tags and symbols. Maia used an alphabet chart to communicate which I held up for her to touch with the tip of her head wand. She spelt out words, which I wrote down. She selected different coloured adhesive note tags on which to record the names of herself and the people who were significant from the past and present.

When placing the tags onto the relationship map (Figure 3.1) we needed to allow enough space for symbolic objects, which would be chosen and added at the next session. We placed her own name tag at a central point and then added people one by one as they came into her mind. Under her direction, some people were placed in close proximity to her own name tag at the centre of the map, whereas others were placed at the outer edge, which was, however, nearer to her actual physicality. Still others were placed halfway to the edge of the map on the furthest diagonal. I was aware of some of the unrequited dimensions of her relationships, and yet she arrived at what appeared to be a very grounded and realistic layout of her relationships as they currently stood.

Once this process was completed, we taped down the note tags permanently so that the map could be used over a series of sessions. At the next session, Maia set about the task of choosing appropriate symbols for each of the name tags. Unexpectedly, when the symbol work was near completion, new names came to light that needed to be included. These people had not previously been discussed in therapy and were key to the unexplored traumatic event.

The relationship map became a story board through which Maia could share undisclosed events that had taken place 15 years earlier. It took willingness and perseverance on both of our parts to reach an understanding of the information. Communication was slower than would have been the case with a person who could directly verbalise, as Maia had to spell out words one letter at a time using her spell chart and head wand.

Figure 3.1 Example of a relationship map using name tags and symbols (see insert for colour version)

There had been aspects of what had taken place revealed previously, however, in a way that was disconnected from the context. This was because Maia had not been able to remember the full sequence of events. At times there had also been public outbursts of rage and frustration related to the events. Even with some prior knowledge, what she shared came as a shock and it was painful to contemplate. As her therapist I was aware that, "In any relationship in which the goal is positive change on the part of the client, being fully present is a fundamental aspect of effective work" (McAdams 1993, p.70). Her account was so detailed that this put an end to the question, "How could this happen?" and she left the session in an emotionally calm state, reassured that someone else now knew what had happened and the impact that this had made on her life.

Session 3: Reading and fully contextualising events of the story board

In session 3, Maia arrived with many unanswered questions about the circumstances surrounding the traumatic events. We reconstructed the relationship map from photographs taken at the end of session 2 as a touchstone from which to move forward. The events needed to be put into a historical cultural context in order for her to fully understand them. We also spent time researching on the Internet to find photographs of the geographical location in which the events took place. We looked at human anatomy and physiology as it relates to people in general and also her own experiences. We then talked about rituals that are used culturally in saying goodbye to people.

In planning for the next session, we conceptualised the making of a fitting tribute to a particular person whose significance and loss had never been fully acknowledged. We also planned a lakeside ceremony where we could allow the tribute to float away in peace and beauty. Significantly, the person whose loss she would be commemorating was not the person identified at the point of referral.

Session 4: Creating a tribute and holding a ritual ceremony
Part 1: In the Arts therapy room
Pearson (1991) stated, "Rituals can be used in healing or transformation…as a way of focusing attention on the transformation desired and focusing the consciousness…on letting go of the former reality and welcoming in the desired new reality" (p.202). It was important that the tribute and ritual reflected the cultural background and preferences of Maia, who identified as bicultural Māori and New Zealand European. *Harakeke* (flax) weaving was an appropriate basis for the tribute with regard to her Māori roots. Flowers were recognised as motifs of funeral rites, worship and celebrations globally, including rituals associated with her Christian beliefs.

Flowers and foliage had been gathered from various sources to present her with multiple choices. We discussed possibilities of shape, size and so forth for the finished tribute before beginning the weaving of *harakeke* and floral construction. As we created the tribute piece by piece under her creative direction, we also talked about the significance of using a ritual and what this might mean in terms giving recognition to her experiences. We talked about how this had the potential to bring healing and how it could also honour her spiritual beliefs.

Once the tribute was completed, Maia asked to revisit the symbols that she had chosen to represent the people involved in the events, either by knowledge or participation. After spending time viewing them again, she indicated that she was ready to perform the ritual.

Part 2: At the lakeside
"There are universal characteristics in all rites of passage and rites of restoration. One of them is the practice of leaving the everyday situation and entering into a devotional space for a period of time" (Knill *et al.* 2005, p.77).

We had arranged to meet at a nearby lake later in the day to hold the ceremony. She arrived by taxi and, as is so often the case for people with disabilities, the time limit would be briefer than the ideal due to the external factors, in this case the taxi schedule. With the tribute carefully and discreetly contained in a box, we found an ideal place at the lake edge to perform the ritual privately. Uncovering the tribute, we again made acknowledgements of the people who had knowledge of the events or who had been directly involved, and of Maia's spiritual beliefs.

When she was ready, I placed the tribute in the water naming the person it commemorated, and it floated (Figure 3.2). There was a great sense of peace as Maia watched in a mesmerised state as it moved slowly away, out onto the lake. It seemed that we could have both stayed watching it drifting all afternoon had her taxi not arrived so promptly to collect her.

Figure 3.2 A similar smaller-sized tribute being released into water (see insert for colour version)

Session 5: Debrief

At session 5, we viewed photographs taken of the tribute floating on the lake and reviewed the ceremony. I offered my observations that she had seemed very peaceful as the tribute drifted away and suggested that she might have made gains in how she was now feeling. She admitted that it had brought some sense of peace; however, she was reluctant to agree that it had been helpful in any other way. This seemed to be related to a fear of completion, of things ending and resulting in abandonment. When I persevered, asking again if there had been any changes, she initially said "no"; however, she then began to nod and smile in acknowledgement. I suggested that this might have been like "a piece of a jigsaw puzzle fitting into place" and that potentially she might feel a greater sense of wholeness. There was a breakthrough as she smiled broadly, nodding and vocalising "yes!"

Upon her request, we then revisited the relationship map, laying out all of the symbols once more so that there could be a full recap. Once she was satisfied, I offered options for how she might progress further through using other media in the next session, and she asked if she could make a painting on canvas.

Session 6: Painting on canvas
Maia painted part of her experience related to the events and the effect that it had had on her as a person, which successfully brought a full sense of completion. She asked that I now share her journey with her psychologist, and if I could also help her share what had taken place with a woman who had become a trusted friend and mentor.

Session 7: Sharing her experience with her mentor
Lubin and Johnson (2008) stated, "Often after the traumatic event the victim experiences a real or perceived rejection by…[their] support system and society… The audience, as representatives of society at large, can thus offer…a positive homecoming experience through their presence, respect and support" (p.89). We met with her mentor a month later in a café that Maia had chosen. Naturally we needed to find a quiet, private corner in order to explain the traumatic occurrences of the past and how she had brought closure to this through her arts therapy journey. Her mentor was compassionate, affirmed that the things which had happened were wrong and celebrated that Maia would now be able to move forward in her life anew. Being in the café helped to anchor the experience as a homecoming by offering an environment of vibrant, everyday community life where celebration naturally flowed from the sharing.

Summary
The six-session process began with the notion of creating a relationship map using name tags and symbols. This effectively brought an area of unresolved trauma and grief into focus, and the use of the rituals of commemoration and homecoming were used as a means of healing

and transformation. The archetypal approaches brought closure to traumatic events that had been troubling the client for 15 years.

Case study: Fairy Garden
Client background

Jamie was a woman in her 20s who had cerebral palsy and received very high needs (VHN) funding due to the severity of her condition. She was unable to walk and used a manual wheelchair. She was dependent on others to assist her with all aspects of daily living and mobility and was considered to be non-verbal. She also had epilepsy, which had an impact on her arts therapy sessions. She had full upper-body and upper-limb movement; however, coordination of a paintbrush was difficult for her. She attended art therapy as a means of enhancing her wellbeing and to gain personal fulfilment through the avenues of communication and creativity that the sessions provided.

She had a close relationship with her parents, who had helped to establish her flatting situation in supported accommodation with other people of a similar age who had disabilities. She had a twin sister, Jessie, who did not have a disability, with whom she was very close. She had another sister, a brother and grandparents, who were also important in her life.

Art therapy overview

Art therapy for the fairy garden project took place through weekly (or sometimes fortnightly) sessions over the course of nine months, where there were two interruptions of six weeks while she participated in exhibitions. The process took part in four stages:

1. Web researching fairy gardens
2. Creating a collage design
3. Working with a simultaneous process of creating the elements and painting responses
4. Making meaning of the archetypal journey of the fairies in the paintings

There was also an unplanned project extension—"Visioning your future for the year ahead"—incorporating photos of her own fairy garden.

History through arts therapy programme

Jamie had begun attending arts therapy sessions after she left special-needs school at 21 years of age and had worked with the arts therapist and interns at the rehabilitation centre for six years. Through her VHN funding, Jamie had access to long-term individual art therapy. This was considered to be a very positive means of self-expression which helped her to maintain emotional wellbeing.

Another significant contribution that attending art therapy made to her life was the avenue to express her cultural interests and personal preferences and to formulate goals. Jamie was considered to be non-verbal with communication taking place primarily through body language, facial expressions and eye movements; gleeful sounds, laughter and sometimes clapping indicated her pleasure, affirmation or approval. On one occasion, she spontaneously sang a line in a song that we were listening to while painting, and in music group which she also attended, she would vocalise tune sounds once the words were familiar to her.

Although Jamie had good upper-limb movement, she found coordination using a paintbrush challenging. She would use a paintbrush independently for brief periods before seeking to use my hand as an extension of its handle in order to give herself more control. I would also assist her to dip her brush into the paint trays as she selected her colour preferences, which she signalled with her eyes.

Jamie had epilepsy and could have as many as six seizures within a 45-minute period of active engagement. They were usually between 30 seconds and 2 minutes long. Upon regaining consciousness, she would experience a surge of almost euphoric energy, often grabbing the paintbrush to engage in vigorous mark-making which she clearly enjoyed.

Art therapy seemed to allow her to move beyond disability and into the realm of greater wholeness and empowered wellbeing, which she confirmed through her participation in 5-Pt Star self-evaluation (see Chapter 2). This provided a range of choices about the benefits of attending art therapy, through which she was able to convey that it helped her to feel emotionally calmer, more positive, better understood and happier in her life. She had also found fulfilment and meaning through the aesthetic qualities of her works and through opportunities to produce art on canvases for exhibitions. Outcomes had included sales of paintings and receiving a competition award, which provided rare moments of public recognition of her strengths and abilities.

Overview of interventions and outcomes

One of Jamie's favourite ways of creating artworks was to choose an A2 sheet of coloured paper that reflected her mood on the day. Using an easel, she would paint to the rhythms of upbeat music using colours and mark-making which further extended her expression of mood. We would then spend time looking through magazines together and I would watch the level of interest in her facial expressions and eye movements. When her eyes came to rest on something, it usually indicated that she would like it to be cut out and put to one side. After choosing a range of images, she would then indicate placement through choosing from a series of compositional possibilities, or she would indicate where she wanted it placed by the direction of her eyes on the painting. Next, she would choose from the mixed-media resource boxes of glitter, ribbons, fabric, beads and scrapbooking embellishments with placement of these items arrived at in a similar way. At the end of the session, we would reflect together on the symbolism and the overall effect.

The fairy garden project came about through this process, where she had chosen a photograph of a fairy garden from a magazine as one of the images for her mixed-media artwork. The fascination and focus that her gaze held when viewing the image indicated that this was something beyond the usual. As I paused and observed her interest, I asked if this was something she would perhaps like to create. Her chin lifted and her eyebrows were clearly raised, and her hands came together in a clap. I suggested that we could email her support team so that this could be added to her goal plans, initially thinking that she might work on the project with support at home; however, later it became clear that art therapy would be the most appropriate place in which to create a "living work of art."

Arts therapy sessions

Stage 1: Web researching fairy gardens

Jamie and I began the journey toward creating a "living work of art" within the fairy garden genre by doing Web searches for images through Google. This revealed an extensive photographic collection from which she was able to select and print out those which held interest. From this we cut out the elements that she most liked and discussed possible variations such as colour schemes, materials, scale and preferred types of plants.

Stage 2: Creating a collage design

From the Web search, Jamie had decided to use a large terracotta pot as a container. We created a circular collage to scale through making colour photocopy enlargements of her selected elements and experimenting with the placement of them.

Stage 3: Working with a simultaneous process of creating the elements and painting responses

The construction of the fairy garden involved a multimedia approach whereby I was Jamie's technician for the parts she could not construct herself. Wherever possible, she took some hands-on involvement in construction, and she painted most of the elements herself. The fairies were made from a sculpting medium which was baked at a low oven heat. Their paint work involved using masking tape to contain the paint and create the careful detail of skin tone and clothing. The fairy shelter required the use of hard board and a jigsaw. Other elements were made from heavy cardboard and layers of PVA glue. Everything was varnished to create waterproofing. The completed fairy garden is shown in Figures 3.3 and 3.4.

Alongside the making of the fairy garden elements, painting took place on paper, both as a means of her designing the details and in response to the process. As the project emerged, Jamie established a ritual of painting "the fairies dancing in the garden" in the final part of each session. As a therapist, I became the witness to a parallel journey which aroused my curiosity and was greatly thought provoking. Her self-directed paintings were possibly more significant on a therapeutic level than the creation of the fairy garden in all its different aspects.

Figure 3.3 Completed fairy garden (see insert for colour version)

Figure 3.4 Fairies in their garden

Stage 4: Making meaning of the archetypal journey of the fairies in the paintings

In terms of Erickson's theory of human development, in young adulthood from 20–40 years (Jamie's age group), "Energies are focused on intimate relationships, learning to live with [a] marriage partner, starting a family, managing a home" (Weiten 2004, p.464). Jamie had displayed interest in this developmental stage in some of her previous collages, where she would often include images of romantically involved couples and weddings. Creating the fairy pairing seemed to be a continuation of this; however, her painting series (Figure 3.5) seemed to indicate that something more could be taking place at a deeper level of her psyche.

McAdams (1993) suggests that in childhood fairy tales "speak softly and subtly…promoting growth and adaptation" encouraging children "to face the world with confidence and hope" (p.31); also, that a child "dwells on images" adapting them to their own imagination beyond the fairy story that has been told, and that in adulthood we construct personal mythology in a similar way (p.53).

Fairies are archetypal and found in the histories of many different cultures. In Western culture, images of fairies seem to return us to that enchanted childhood place, one of suspended reality where butterflies can be tiny human beings that carry special messages. They can live freely in their paradise under large leaves, perched on top of flowers, and float in seed-pod boats in complete harmony with nature. Theirs is a world of sanctuary and peace, filled with the possibility of magical transformation, which might sometimes include mischief. All of these dimensions seemed to be present for Jamie within the therapeutic space in the imaginative, joyful and playful way that she engaged.

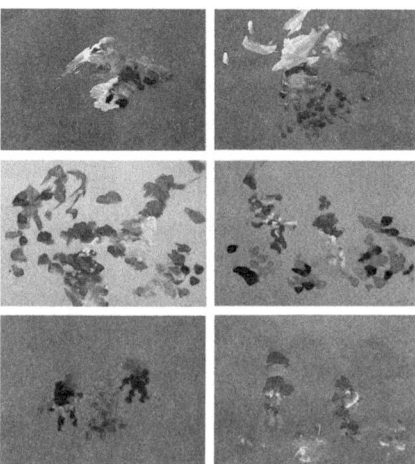

Figure 3.5 Series of paintings "fairies in their garden" (see insert for colour version)

In the first painting that she spontaneously created to begin the series, the fairies appeared to be in physical contact, becoming overlapped and immersed. In witnessing the composition being created, it was clear that these were two separate moving figures, although this was not clear in the completed painting. As the painting ritual unfolded session by session, I noticed that there was a progressive separation of the two figures and growth in the space between them within the compositions.

I began to ponder on Jung's theories of animus, that a woman carries a male counterpart within her who is frequently present in dreams and can become accessible to the conscious mind. "Her animus can turn into an invaluable inner companion…[providing her with] the qualities of, courage, objectivity and spiritual wisdom" (Jung 1964, p.194). He also theorised the process of individuation as being "the consciousness coming to terms with one's own center or Self" toward maturity (1964, p.166). "Separation and individuation are two parallel processes of development during adolescence" (Meeus *et al.* 2005, p.89). Both of Jung's theoretical notions held possibilities toward Jamie's self-directed painting process, and although she was post-adolescent, there had been an assessment made in another context that she was developmentally delayed and still emotionally pre-pubescent.

Another perspective to be considered was that she had a close relationship with her twin sister, Jessie. It was possible that she was coming to terms with their adult state of having now established different lifestyles in localities further apart from each other.

From an archetypal perspective, Siemon (1980) stated, "Twins have had special significance and played an important role in the mythology of almost all ancient and primitive cultures. Twins have been heroes and demigods, or imbued with magical powers" (p.387). In terms of twins separating:

> The extent of differentiation, and the degree of difficulty experienced… depends on the kind of relationship that twins have had with each other and feelings they have about being a twin. Whether or not twins are genetically identical is not as important an influence on separation experiences as twins' perceptions of similarity. (p.388)

When Jamie painted the sixth painting in the series shown in Figure 3.5, I had the sense through witnessing her mark-making that one of the two fairies might be moving away from the other. Finally, I raised the twinhood topic with her saying, "I am wondering if the two fairies also have something to do with Jamie and Jessie, the twins?"

I knew from past experience that if my suggestion was off track, this would have been met by silence, stillness and absolutely no reaction; however, this offering gained one of the occasional squeals of delight accompanied by a clap, which let me know I was definitely onto something. "It looks to me as if one fairy is about to fly out of the painting, and the other is staying." Exuberant laughter was her response, encouraging me to explore further. "Is this perhaps what happens with you and Jessie? She goes away and comes back, and that is okay for her to do?" Nods, smiles, more laughter. Clearly, with that line of inquiry, we had arrived somewhere that greatly pleased Jamie and could possibly have helped her to consolidate the process.

It was my impression that the therapeutic process was taking place on multiple levels in a phenomenological way. This was a case of the shaman healer arising from the unconscious of the client to lead the way (McNiff 1992, 2004). Beyond the acknowledgement of her identity as a twin, it seemed unnecessary to explore meaning further, although any or all of the other theoretical perspectives mentioned above may have also been active in her process.

We completed the project by installing her living artwork under her window at home and then taking photographs for her to keep. As we moved into a theme of Christmas, it seemed that the journey was over and that the New Year would bring new direction; however, the fairies returned again as a mode of continued inspiration toward Jamie's future.

Stage 5: "Visioning your future for the year ahead" (incorporating photos of your own fairy garden)

At the beginning of the following year, art therapy clients were offered the opportunity of making pop-up vision boards to carry their aspirations and goals and inspire the way forward (Figures 3.6 and 3.7). For Jamie, the new project came to life when the option of including photos of her fairy garden was included. Options for the shape and design of the pop-up element included different kinds of flowers, birds, animals and symbolic shapes. Jamie chose the heart element, and there seems little need for further narration, as these fairy images can speak for themselves!

Figure 3.6 Vision board cover

Figure 3.7 Vision board internal

Summary and conclusion

Fairies are archetypal symbols which were chosen by the client as a means of self-expression. Creating a fairy garden as a "living work of art" stimulated artistic and technical development as well as therapeutic engagement. The self-directed paintings that emerged in response to the project demonstrated that a deep psychological process was taking place, phenomenologically aiding her transition into adulthood.

In the two case studies of Maia and Jamie, the therapeutic goals and interests were different, and different archetypal approaches emerged through therapeutic engagements that were fitting to their respective situations. Symbols and a ritualistic process were significant for Maia, whereas Jamie set out to create a joyous, living, fairy garden artwork and embarked on a parallel journey of painting. Both individualised pathways led into areas of therapeutic depth and psychological processing, with outcomes that were transformative.

CHAPTER 4

Art Groups

Keywords: multicultural, spirituality, artefacts, found-objects sculpture, storytelling, planning format, goal outcomes

Three arts therapy processes are presented which were developed within groups through person-centred approaches. Each process took a different course in initiation and how it unfolded. "Ancient artefacts" began as a brainstorm leading to Internet research. Focusing questions emerged at different stages that contoured the evolution. "Goddess dolls" employed a questionnaire format that focused the creative therapeutic inquiry and development took place through engagement with mixed media materials. "Sacred vessels" employed research into contemporary fine art and explored the notion of sacredness and generic shapes of cultural and archetypal significance. In each process, the aesthetic was a significant therapeutic aspect, established through art media and key tasks.

Levine (2017) stated:

> aesthetic responsibility has to do with setting up challenging tasks... [in order that participants] have a sense of achievement that moves, touches and amazes—some of the attributes of beauty... [Tasks are posed] that the learner is challenged by and yet able to cope with... focusing on the principal of low skill/ high sensitivity... [This involves] high sensory competency for shaping the artwork and an adequate level of manual skills so that even a non-professional artist can experience the process of art-making. (p.182)

In the context of the groups, people with disabilities demonstrated high sensory competency in imagining and developing the artworks through media choices, and manual tasks were assisted by their support-staff assistants, who included support workers, interns and student volunteers. The arts therapist took the role of monitoring collaborations to ensure that they were client led and maximised clients' abilities. In reviewing the outcomes, the artworks held integrity for the primary art makers.

Hosli and Wanzeried (2017, p.192) have provided a model for working therapeutically within an educational context with an emphasis on learning and, at the same time, accounting for therapeutic needs. The Arts Therapy 5-Pt Star model (see Chapter 2) provided a similar means for ensuring that a balanced process took place in groups. In the context of the art groups, the emphasis was on the therapy and boundaries were set to ensure emotional safety. Individual therapy was possible if issues arose that required further exploration. Archetypal approaches offered encounters through the unconscious that were therapeutically effective and maintained emotional safety; and the aesthetic dimensions added value on multiple levels.

Case study: Ancient civilisations

The theme of ancient civilisations came about through a brainstorm session at the group formation stage with a group of eight people who had physical disabilities and who shared a passion for self-expression through art. The idea of exploring ancient worlds resonated with all present who expressed curiosity and fascination toward the mysteries of past cultures. As the arts therapist, I did not immediately make a connection with the highly significant archetypal dimensions. I was willing to follow the lead of the group and see where it would take us.

We set out on a journey of Internet research to discover images of artefacts and symbols that related to the long-ago histories of different ethnicities relevant to individual group members (Figure 4.1). These ethnicities included Celtic, Roman, Greek, Māori, Pacific Island and Chinese cultures, and later Egyptian, Incan and Mayan. Participants selected images to print out and created a personal collage, and then made paintings in response to what they observed, felt and imagined in viewing the compilation. The question that arose for me throughout the first stage of the process was, *How can the ancient symbols and artefacts be made relevant to the personal stories and journeys of the participants?*

Figure 4.1 Research into symbols from ancient civilisations

Connection was made with the Egyptian alphabet as one of the earliest forms of written language, and group members explored their names using hieroglyphic symbols (Figure 4.2). This led to the notion of roles that people who lived in ancient worlds might have held, and vessels and utensils that they might have needed to carry out their roles: "What if we lived in an ancient world and had the job of creating vessels and utensils for significant people, which would later become artefacts in a museum collection? Where might this take us next?"

Figure 4.2 Art by group members in responses to collages and hieroglyphics of name

Resources of plastic bowls, cups and other utensils, and cardboard craft boxes of various shapes and sizes, were presented to the group, along with mixed-media materials (Figure 4.3). The participants needed technical support to make their creations, and it was therefore suggested that they incorporated a sculptural component using air-dried clay, treasures that would be held by the significant person which were moulded entirely by their own hand. Impasto medium, which could be drawn into with minimum assistance, was used on the boxes to create textures and signs. Printouts of their choices from the ancient world research were also integrated to assist with the narrative and decorative process. There were many different media and compositional choices that the participants needed to make in order to arrive at their artefacts.

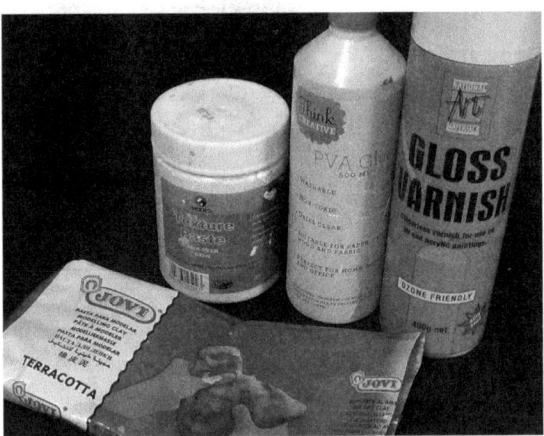

Figure 4.3 Mixed-media products used to transform plastic items into artefacts

There was a profound sense of immersion and engagement in the creative process within the group at each stage of making the artefacts, as if participants had moved through an invisible door into the archetypal dimension, where the ancient world could be recalled and brought back to life. Once completed, there was a sense of awe and astonishment at what had been achieved. As we took time to reflect upon and honour the sacred paths travelled, two questions were posed to shine a light on the significance of what had been made: *Who is it for? What is it used for?* The therapeutic, narrative and aesthetic outcomes of three participants, Rineti, Pauline and Marcus, are presented below.

Outcomes of three participants
Rineti

Rineti, a woman in her early 50s, was very articulate and a great storyteller of her past, particularly about what had been a wonderful childhood with loving parents and a close bond with her sister. Growing up with cerebral palsy had been challenging, even though the family had done everything possible to provide access to the things that would assist her development and lead to a full life. In her adult life, she was challenged by the circumstance of living in supported accommodation with other people who had similar disabilities, and of being in a more marginalised position than she and her family had hoped. She was only able to visit her family once a year at Christmas due to living in a different city, and she had significant bouts of homesickness. She was of English and Scottish descent and knew something of her family heritage. She also belonged to a Māori *iwi* from her hometown area who had given her a Māori name (which she requested be used as her pseudonym). She had happy memories of a holiday in Fiji and was interested in Fijian cultural history.

RINETI'S ANSWERS TO THE KEY QUESTIONS

- *Who is it for?* "The gladiators of Ancient Rome."
- *What is it used for?* "It is ceremonial ladle used by the gladiators to drink medicinal wine after the fight in the victorious ritual" (Figure 4.4).

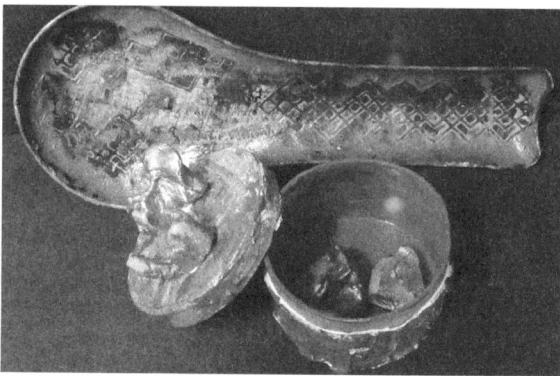

Figure 4.4 Ceremonial victory ladle for the gladiators of Rome with treasure box

In making her artefacts, Rineti connected with ancient Rome and was able to explore her personal strength and power, and to bring the part of herself that was a winner of battles to the forefront. Her artefact was used for the purposes of healing and rejuvenation after battles within a public ritual where achievements were cheered and celebrated.

Rineti often found her circumstances to be disempowering, and without the level of practical day-to-day support that her family had provided in earlier life, she did not have access to the same level of opportunities. There were daily battles in an effort to establish a meaningful and productive adult life. Her art was an area of skill and talent where she was able to share her stories and advocate for disability awareness and greater inclusion, which she did through participating in exhibitions and producing self-published illustrated books. Her art metaphorically provided the victorious public rituals and moments of healing through being recognised and affirmed. The journey of making, naming and celebrating her artefacts was one where she was able to experience a period of personal triumph, which enhanced self-esteem.

Pauline

Pauline, who was in her early 50s, was also living with the challenges of cerebral palsy. She was verbally able, with the additional challenges of a developmental disorder. Unlike Rineti, she had never known her family and had no knowledge of her ancestry, and she identified as being bicultural in European and Māori cultures. Her conversations were often related to the experience of chronic pain, health concerns and anxieties related to her safety. She was dependent on support staff to transfer her using a hoist every time she needed to move from her wheelchair. Skill was required on behalf of the staff in using the hoist and occasionally she was bumped against things, and she feared being dropped.

She lived in supported accommodation and had developed some sense of family within the community of staff, some of whom made extra efforts to support her interests and even took her home on Christmas Day. She had also formed attachments to her flatmates who had disabilities; however, there were losses through death and people moving to other facilities. There was also sometimes bullying among residents which created anxieties.

PAULINE'S ANSWERS TO THE KEY QUESTIONS

- *Who is it for?* "An Egyptian prince."
- *What is it used for?* "A vessel to hold gold coins, kept safely at the prince's bedside" (Figure 4.5).

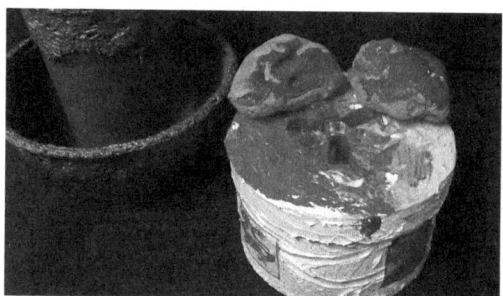

Figure 4.5 Vessel to hold gold coins for a prince, and a treasure box with treasures displayed

In creating her artefacts, Pauline stayed with the connections she had made through the Egyptian hieroglyphics of her name and explored the esteemed role of a prince. She found a way of providing safety for the prince's treasures, which would enable him to sleep peacefully and free from worries. Pauline had connected with her princely self, the part that was noble, empowered and held gold. There was a parallel between a prince's life and her own in that both needed trustworthy people to assist and protect them. Through the journey of artefacts creation, she was able to identify and claim her need for peace of mind, to be able to act and rest with greater confidence, while also acknowledging her own intrinsic worth.

Marcus

Marcus was a man in his 40s who had cerebral palsy and an intellectual disability. He had regular contact with family who lived in the same city, and he made a point of keeping in touch with others who lived further away. He took a strong interest in the construction industry including making regular visits to local sites to witness different stages of progress in the construction of new buildings, and he watched videos on YouTube of construction taking place. He was a keen painter with an intuitive understanding of colour and composition, and frequently made paintings as gifts for family and support staff.

Marcus identified with both European and Māori cultures and had a strong appreciation of the Niuean culture of one of his male flatmates. Social settings could be challenging for him and he had individual support in attending the group.

MARCUS'S ANSWERS TO THE KEY QUESTIONS

- *Who is it for?* "A great chief."
- *What is it used for?* "The chief would eat his *hangi* [food cooked using the traditional Māori technique with hot stones in the ground] from it. When not in use, it was the place where his pet snake would sleep" (Figure 4.6).

Figure 4.6 Dual-purpose bowl of a chief for eating hangi *and keeping his pet snake*

Marcus's artefact was a bowl for a great chief who ate *hangi*. His box held an image, on the inside, of a chief navigating the oceans in a traditional Fijian vessel (Figure 4.7), and his sculptural element was a snake.

Figure 4.7 Inside the treasure box was the photo of a chief navigating the seas (see insert for colour version)

Marcus had created artefacts which brought the notions of dignified empowerment and self-control to life. There were archetypal references to having mastery over one's self as is expected of a chief; and also in the face of the unpredictable elements of the wild, which were present in both the snake who sleeps openly in a bowl and the chief sailing a boat in all kinds of weather on high seas. There was also a sense of utilising intuitive knowledge in the snake, and in the chief navigating journeys by the stars.

In archetypal terms, the snake or serpent was a symbol of goddesses in the ancient worlds, "giver of food and eternal life" (Walker 1988, p.388). This offered the suggestion that the food consumed by the chief might go beyond that of the earthly world, and also that Marcus was balancing the masculine and the feminine within his artwork.

Museum posters were developed to hold the stories of the artefacts which would be exhibited at events (Figure 4.8). There was a great sense of achievement and pleasure in having created objects of aesthetic beauty and significance, which had been conceptualised and created to represent each person's own uniqueness and self-worth. The posters further proclaimed their value.

Figure 4.8 Museum poster to accompany the artefact exhibits when displayed

Group reflections through discussion upon completion of project

"What has been the value of exploring ancient civilisations?"

"There was a sense of wonder and of being drawn into the spiritual, a sense of sacredness."

"Why was this the case?"

- The mystery and beliefs of their lifestyles
- The origins of Christianity and other religions
- Travel by stars and navigation using handcrafted vessels
- The origins of written language

"It was a reminder of my great, great grandparents who came to New Zealand in early 1800s. I don't know as much about them as I would like and want to find out more. There is some mystery about them."

"The mystery of the ancient cultures drew us in and we wanted to know about them, so it helped to fill in the gaps in what we know about our own heritage."

"I was able to express how I feel about Christianity and I want to give my treasure box to one of my teachers from Church who lost a family member recently. It has a picture of baby Jesus inside it."

"It relates back to the beginning of the Bible and how Moses was rescued by a servant girl and then adopted into the Pharaoh's family."

"The things held inside the box have meaning only when the box is opened and when they are taken out of the box. The significance is personal to the person who made them."

Summary

Our exploration of ancient civilisations was a journey into the realms of both the familiar and the unknown, led by the curiosity and therapeutic needs of a group of eight people who had physical disabilities. The processes which evolved reconnected us with origins of both written language and artmaking. Gombrich (1979) stated:

> There is a direct tradition, handed down from master to pupil, and from pupil to admirer or copyist, which links art of our own days, any house or any poster, with the art of the Nile Valley of some five thousand years ago…the Greek masters went to school with the Egyptians, and we are all pupils of the Greeks. (p.31)

In the case studies of Rineti, Pauline and Marcus as representatives of the group, each person's process brought focus symbolically to an area of their lives that they had been struggling with, which brought a greater sense of control, competency and fulfilment.

Jung (1964, pp.20–21) stated:

> A word or image is symbolic when it implies something more than the obvious and immediate meaning. It has a wider "unconscious" aspect that is never precisely defined or fully explained. No one can hope to define or explain it. As the mind explores the symbol, it is led to ideas that lie beyond the grasp of reason.

Reconnecting with ancient cultures opened windows within the soul that allowed the entry of factors that brought about greater self-knowledge, spirituality and social connection, and the sense of having been bequeathed a great shared inheritance, which enhanced wellbeing and self-esteem.

Case study: Goddess dolls

The making of goddess dolls brought together two concepts: of arts as therapeutic and that of archetypal significance. Dolls were an interactive symbol of self and a point of connection with goddesses within oneself. The planning process brought the notion of goddess to life and the resourcing process made the approaches accessible for people with physical disabilities with technical assistance. Goddess doll creations took place in groups and in individual sessions, from which case examples and outcomes are presented.

Feen-Calligan, McIntyre and Sands-Goldstein (2011) stated:

> The cultural and historical roles of dolls help explain their appeal in art therapy: In history and in art therapy dolls are symbols for ourselves or for something greater…they teach and have power… stimulate the imagination…have the potential to speak and to provide companionship. (p.172)

Table 4.1 provides a selective summary of the historical uses and contexts provided.

Table 4.1 Historical use of dolls

Cultural context	Use of dolls
Ancient Greece and Rome	Girls played with dolls until married, then deposited them at the shrines of the goddess chosen to protect them.
Africa	Young Ashanti women carried dolls to dispel infertility.
Nineteenth-century America	Doll role-plays helped girls learn about grief and mourning etiquette.
Thailand	The Ramakien dolls were used to tell the story of the rescue of a princess.
Native America	Kachina dolls were used as a teaching tool about the spirits by Native American Hopi.
Bali	Dolls were created to honour the rice goddess Dewi Sri.

From Feen-Calligan, McIntyre and Sands-Goldstein (2011, p.167)

Bolen (1985) stated, "When a woman senses that there is a mythical dimension to something she is undertaking, that knowledge touches and inspires deep creative centres in her" (p.6). "In ancient Greece, women knew that their vocation or their stage of life placed them under the domain of a particular goddess… Within contemporary women, the goddesses exist as archetypes" (p.25). The goddess dolls produced demonstrated inspired creativity and archetypal wisdom, which supported the therapeutic and personal goals of the participants.

Gordon-Flower (2014a) provided the case study of Petra, a woman who had a disability and was recovering from post-traumatic stress disorder (PTSD) after being involved in the Christchurch, New Zealand, earthquake of 22 February 2011. One of the interventions which aided her recovery was the creation of her own goddess, "a doll… imbued with special transforming powers, capable of helping people and the world" (p.43). Petra had been struggling with the experience of having conflicting emotions and was seeking the confidence to rejoin the "dance of life." She created "Karen, the dancing, singing, laughing, giggling goddess" capable of carrying and expressing a full range of emotions (pp.43–44). This successfully completed her art therapy of four months, as she was then able to move forward in her life.

Campbell (1976) stated, "The first function of mythology is to reconcile the waking consciousness to the *mysterium tremendum et fascirians* of this universe *as it is*" (p.4). The Latin term translates as "a mystery before which man both trembles and is fascinated, is both repelled and attracted" (Encyclopaedia Britannica 2018). Campbell (1976, pp.4–5) suggested that mythology has three key functions within psyche:

- To reconcile the beauty and brutality present in the mysteries of the universe

- To "mirror" them in a way that can be accepted by the "contemporary conscious mind"

- To create "moral" and social order within a "geographical and historical" context

In the case of Petra, she was struggling to reconcile the mass destruction caused by the earthquake. She was seeking to find the beauty, which she believed to be potentially present in her life. The need to create order from chaos was being addressed on a geographical and national level, and on a personal level, Petra sought to regain a sense of order within her emotions (Gordon-Flower 2014a, pp.33–47). Goddesses offered the notion of female empowerment beyond the frailties of our human vulnerability and mortality, which she was able to utilise to her therapeutic benefit.

The goddess dolls brought opportunities for participants in "Women Together" groups and individual sessions, as they were able to utilise the approaches relevant to their own needs and life interests. In group settings, there was the added social benefit. Feen-Calligan *et al.* (2011) stated:

> One benefit from making dolls in groups is the enhancement of a person's sense of self with the help of others who provide feedback. This derives from the theory of symbolic interaction—that personal identity is formed in large part through interactions with others. (p.167)

Group process in creating personalised goddesses

Women who used the service had been introduced to *Goddess Guidance Oracle Cards* (Virtue 2004) "from both ancient and modern cultures and religions, including the Greek, Roman, Egyptian, Mayan, African, Christian, Tibetan, and Buddhist" (p.8). Each card provided a goddess image with a positive message. These were sometimes used at the beginning of the session where each woman, including staff, would choose one as a means of self-reflection toward how the wise words it held might apply. As each person shared their card with the group, there was an honouring of their intrinsic value and worthiness to receive the goddess message. This brought about a sense of unity and also successfully transitioned the dining area into a sacred or therapeutic space to be held and maintained by the arts therapist (Moon 2002). Cards were referred to again at the end of the session as a means of transition toward returning to everyday life.

With the notion of creating personalised goddesses, a format was developed to facilitate their materialisation which focused on key aspects of goddesshood:

- Physical appearance
- Magic powers
- Special tools and equipment
- Ability to help the world
- Naming of the goddess
- Catch-phrase descriptor

The dolls were all approximately 20 centimetres high, with medium-length hair of blond or black, pale skin tone and blue eyes—features which could easily be changed with paint. They were naked apart from shoes and hair ribbons, which provided a blank canvas. There was the potential to cut, dye and/or extend the hair. These dolls were not grown-up in their shape as in "Barbie," or strong as in action figures or sophisticated as in China dolls; however, the goddesses were yet to be conceived and born into the attributed gifts. These somewhat naïve dolls were very well suited to the tasks of conception, birth and transformation.

The invitation of the doll canvas waiting to be filled in, and the potential adaptability of features, inspired the imaginations of the goddess creators and their staff assistants. After working with the planning format, most participants began the art process by painting a new skin tone. Colours chosen included black, browns from dark to olive, metallic gold and bronze. Eye colours were also changed. Once personalised in her naked form, she was then clothed in glory and gifted with her special equipment, tools and powers, through which she would be able to help the world.

An array of fabrics, ribbons, laces and brocades provided almost endless possibilities of how the goddesses might be dressed. Experimentation with colour schemes, textures and garment construction led to the desired expression of goddess persona. Magazine photographs, cardboard, wire, skewer sticks, beads, glues and other materials were used in creating the special equipment and tools. Once completed to the satisfaction of the artist, they were celebrated as having been imbued with their powers.

In other contexts, it might be possible to make fabric dolls; however, this did not present as a practical option for the client group with physical disabilities. Stace (2014) provided a case study of a woman recovering from PTSD who created a series of six dolls using "[a]different technique for each doll in her series…each doll's design [was] noteworthy; her choice of materials and technique were significant in creating…[a] body of artwork on which to build personal meaning" (p.14).

There were obvious benefits, at the time, from the positivity that arrived through creative engagement, and of increased self-esteem through creating an object of beauty with powers that were self-reflective. In group settings, the women learned to appreciate each other more as the uniqueness and appeal of each goddess were recognised. There were also benefits which took longer to manifest in terms of how the goddesses had helped their creators to employ strengths within themselves. Eventually there were clear reflections of their goddesses as being "present and at work" in their lives.

Case examples and comparison

In addition to Petra (Gordon-Flower 2014a), two women who carried goddess powers into their lifestyles with observable outcomes were Maia and Leanne. (Maia contributed to a case study presented in Chapter 3.) The goddess doll-making process took place at an earlier time, when she attended the home-based "Women Together" group. This explored the interests of four women flatmates living in supported accommodation with 24 hours assistance and included the theme of needing to get along with each other within conditions that were sometimes very difficult. They created their goddess dolls together with staff assistance, through which they learned more about each other within the safety and support of the arts therapy space. Leanne, who was in her mid-40s, also attended a group with her flatmates which focused more directly on strategies for positive living and conflict resolution, which was held at an external venue rather than being home-based. Alongside the group, Leanne was offered the opportunity to create her goddess through individual sessions.

Maia and Leanne both had cerebral palsy, however, with different challenges. Maia used a communication device or spell chart with her head wand to speak, and was unable to move her arms and hands independently. She used a paintbrush strapped to her head wand in art therapy, and employed this system with a pen to write her signature. She had recently acquired a new head-controlled motorised wheelchair which she was learning to drive. Leanne, on the other hand, was verbally articulate and had upper-limb mobility, although with some limitations in hand function. She used a motorised wheelchair with hand controls. Both of them needed practical assistance at each stage of the doll-making process. Despite the physical challenges they each faced, using the goddess-creation process gave birth to life-changing visions which formed the basis of the much bigger lives that they came to lead.

The makings of a goddess

Table 4.2 provides a comparison of the following:

- How Maia and Leanne each employed the format and process
- How this supported the development and achievement of goals
- Observations of goddess attributes active within their lives

Table 4.2 Step 1: Format questionnaire

Focusing questions	Maia's response	Leanne's response
Skin colour	Brown	Olive
Hair colour	Black	Blond
Colour of eyes	Hazel	Pink

Magic powers	She is the goddess of beauty and happiness.	She is positive, has a sense of humour and sings.
Special tools and equipment	She carries a smile.	She wears jewels and a hat, carries a torch to fix things and carries a computer.
How does she help the world?	Everywhere she goes she lights up the world.	She helps people find the right place to live.
What is her name?	Maia	Cinderella
How is she best described?	All around her is stardust and moonlight.	She is a singing goddess and very smart.

The naming of the goddesses proved therapeutically significant. On a personal level, Maia was working to overcome grief and symptoms of PTSD related to past events. In naming her goddess "Maia," she made a recognition that change needed to come from herself rather than externally, and also identified a positive strength that she already had in the ability to connect through her smile. In the case of Leanne, under the circumstances of her living situation, "Cinderella" was a very fitting name choice. This was a fairy-tale character who was displaced in her home life; however, through interventions of a fairy godmother and a prince, transformation took place bringing about new living arrangements and lifestyle changes, for which Leanne held similar hopes (Tables 4.3 and 4.4).

Table 4.3 Step 2: Changing the skin tone, eye colour and hairstyle

	Maia's response	Leanne's response
Skin tone	To reflect Māori ancestry and ancient cultural history	Colour mixing using metallic gold, bronze and white for olive tone with resonant sheen
	Colour mixing to create appropriate brown	Mostly painted by an assistant due to hand-function difficulties
	Painted using head wand and arm extended/hand supported by assistant	
Eye colour	Careful intervention to create hazel eye colour under her direction	Pink and gold used in the eye colour change under her direction
Hair	Considered suitable in existing style	Considered suitable (to be partly covered by hat at next stage)

Table 4.4 Step 3: Goddess clothing and special equipment

	Maia's response	Leanne's response
Costuming	She sought out a range of different options in her favourite colours of blue and red.	She experimented with different colour options and textures until arriving at costuming that reflected "smart and savvy" in the contemporary sense.
	She arrived at textures and dress style that suggested an ancient culture.	
Special equipment and tools	Her goddess held a thin wire staff supporting the photo image of a large smile on a card (not shown in photo).	She carried a computer made from a photo image on a card.
	Moonlight and stardust were reflected in the jewels on her costume.	Her bag was the container for her "torch to fix things."

Figure 4.9 shows the goddesses Maia and Cinderella.

Figure 4.9 Goddesses Maia and Cinderella

Outcomes

At the time of creating their goddesses, both Maia and Leanne had begun attending forums specifically for goal setting and skill building toward employment. Maia had identified an interest in working with children. Leanne was committed to becoming an advocate for social change and also had an interest in working with children. Although lifestyle goals were not discussed in connection with the goddess dolls, it became evident that links had been unconsciously made. Under the circumstances of the prevailing societal attitudes, these goals were not easy to voice as they were mostly thought to be unrealistic. The goddesses provided an avenue through which to articulate in a different way, which proved to be "goal activating."

Due to her dysarthria, Maia needed a way to engage beyond words in order to build relationships which could assist in reaching her goals. Her goddess of beauty and happiness—"Maia, who carries a smile and everywhere she goes, lights up the world, surrounded by moondust and starlight"—brought to life the necessary persona for the life she was seeking to lead. As opportunities arose to meet with people who could assist, her smile became a key point of power and connection, frequently commented upon by others. She gained a volunteer job role as a teacher aide as her presence was recognised as motivating to children. She was able to lead paintings sessions with assistance and provided live demonstrations and PowerPoint presentations using her communication device, which could be pre-programmed to talk. She initiated collaborations between schools where 11-year-old children read books aloud for children with profound disabilities, and she became an occasional disability awareness presenter.

Leanne's goddess—"Cinderella, who is a singing goddess, very smart and positive with a sense of humour, wears jewels and a hat, carries a computer, and finds people the right place to live"—provided a package of qualities, resources and attributes that Leanne was able to adopt and successfully utilise. She applied for a grant to purchase a laptop and then found tuition and ongoing practical assistance at a local library. She was appointed to an advisory committee for a disability organisation and became a skilled disability awareness presenter at community events. She was recognised for her soprano voice and performed both on- and off-stage leadership roles in a choir group. She also became a volunteer teacher aide in schools, assisting children with disabilities in reading, singing, expressive movement and art.

Summary

The cases of Petra, Maia and Leanne demonstrated how three women each utilised the goddess-doll format and processes in a different way to support their therapeutic needs and lifestyle goals. There was a phenomenological dimension in how this took place related to the archetypal approach, which allowed the unconscious mind to be the director in the required steps. When provided in group settings, this intervention offered additional benefits through the affirming social dimensions which were created.

Case study: Sacred vessels

In "sacred vessels" the notion of containers that held precious cargo and travelled on water was explored as a beginning point, arriving at places that were more individualised. There was also an exploration of what constitutes "the sacred" and how this could nurture self-esteem and holistic wellbeing. Artmaking took on rituals through aesthetic processes and visual outcomes brought about strong messages of artistic achievement, competency and esteemed personal identity. The work was exhibited with accompanying art stories, which were met by an appreciative audience. This brought community acknowledgement and helped to reduce the sense of being marginalised. These were building blocks that affirmed social connection and contributed toward confidence and greater wellbeing.

The notion of sacred vessels

The idea of sacred vessels had arrived from contemporary themes within *Aotearoa* (New Zealand) art, where Māori *waka* canoes had inspired sculpture. *Waka* had traditionally been created from ornately carved wood, carvings created to carry the spirits of the ancestors. In terms of carrying precious cargo and *tapu* sacredness, the carvings in themselves qualified as sacred vessels. *Waka* were also used to carry fallen warriors home from battle, which was a highly sacred task. Very large *waka* were the means of travel and migration for Māori and other Pacific cultures who navigated using the stars. In contemporary Māori art, media and design forms were broader and had come to signify the concepts of unity, spirituality and *mana* dignity.

Our European, Māori and Pacific Island cultures shared the influence of Christianity through which there was common knowledge of the Biblical story of a vessel in the water carrying precious cargo in the form of a child. Baby Moses, an Israelite, was placed on the Nile

River in a small covered basket made of reeds and mud. This was for the purposes of hiding him from soldiers who were killing off baby boys, and he was rescued by an Egyptian princess who raised him as her son. The notion of *waka* and sacred vessels held this reference for some of the group.

There were further cultural references that sacred vessels held related to Chinese and Indian cultures. In Auckland where the group was situated, Chinese New Year and Diwali Hindu Festival of Lights had both become high-profile public events celebrated throughout the city. Lanterns were placed on the water as a part of the Chinese New Year to symbolise hopes for a bright future and good fortune. At Diwali, vessels which carried lights symbolised the triumph of good over evil and light over darkness. Both could have potentially been considered by participants within the domain of sacred vessels.

Spirituality was included within the frameworks of our overarching models of practice, which were Person Centred Plan (PCP) and *Te Whare Tapa Whā* (Māori Model for Health). The sacred-vessels initiative provided an opportunity for spiritual exploration, which brought the "essence of Self" or "the soul dimension" into focus in a universal way. West (2011) has suggested that:

> spirituality…in a therapeutic context…[needs to be] rooted in human experience rather than abstract theology…involves linking with other people and the universe at large…faces suffering and its causes…deals with the meaning that people make of their lives…[and] involves non-ordinary consciousness. (pp.16–17)

The aesthetic aspects were strongly considered in the planning and development of objects that needed to reflect sacredness and high value. Through this, the objects could be viewed as having been imbued with the same kind of care, fitting objects used for sacred rites. The end objects were considered maquettes, which in other contexts could have later been made in more permanent materials on a larger scale; however, participants were satisfied with the small-scale models which were practical to take home and treasure.

Having explored the concept of *waka* in contemporary Māori art, the Web research extended into images of other types of vessels from the arts and historical artefacts which could be considered sacred. Conceptual brainstorming in the context of sacred vessels (*waka*) took place with regard to the following aesthetic and narrative considerations:

- Shape and symbolism: egg, little boat, ship, special bowl—square like a house opening at the roof, human form; diamond, triangular, curvy, hexagon (or other geometric shape), star shaped; rockets
- Weight: light, heavy, medium weight, floating
- Materials: paper; glue and construction (wire netting, balloon, light bulbs, can or cane basket materials); metal, stainless steel, tin/aluminium cans; glass, tiles; wood, plastic, rubber, vinyl, fabric, carpet; flowers, pods, gourds
- Colour: earthy, neutral colours, creams and whites, metallic, black, colourful, pastel, multicoloured, monocoloured
- Qualities: fragile, transparent or translucent, sturdy, flat bottom, soft or hard, furry or hairy, spongey, smooth or rough, dainty, large or small
- Other ideas: sink or swim; an opening; multiples of a chosen shape or form

From the brainstorm, participants chose words from each category that would shape their creative exploration. The words chosen guided the selection of materials, which were explored through collages to familiarise with their chosen sculptural shape and test out a range of media options. Colour was explored through monoprinting, stencilling and framing techniques. Most of the final sculptures utilised polystyrene as the primary media.

Three examples of the individualised outcomes
Artist A

- Initial conceptual ideas: egg, medium weight, floating, pink, an opening, flat bottom.
- Drawing process: Artist A tested out colour and shape through monoprints and framing through an egg shape cut into paper (Figure 4.10). She explored a range of media which appealed to her before finalising the materials used in her sculpture.

Figure 4.10 Artist A's testing of shape and media in collage

SCULPTURAL CONSTRUCTION PROCESS

A hollow was carved out on one side of the polystyrene egg, which was also shaved to create a flat bottom. The egg was painted both inside and outside by Artist A. Smooth, shiny shell pieces were glued around the inner edge of the hollow and along the top of the egg. A silk hibiscus flower was inserted into the hollow and the piece was placed on a sea of pink satin. Through the colour use, the flower in the hollow appeared to be glowing (Figure 4.11).

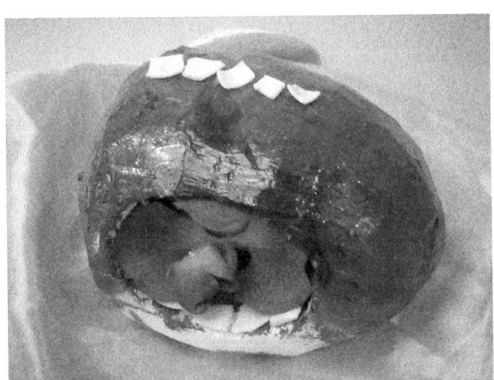

Figure 4.11 Artist A's sacred vessel marquette

The following statement was given by Artist A:

> My sculpture is an egg. I started with pink but then I have painted it using lots of colours. The flower inside my sculpture is about the special things inside of me. A sacred vessel is also a place where I might also store my treasures, like my very special jewellery.

> **Arts therapist's observations**
>
> The artist's concept of medium weight and egg shape suggested the embryo where first life takes form, and which holds the potential of much greater things. The opening provided a view of her inner self, which was delicate and glowing. The painting process extended beyond her original plans in colour scheme and arrived at heavier earth tones, which served to provide a protective layer, making the outer casing appear hard. The shell pieces, although decorative, were hard and durable, placed like a reptilian backbone along the top. Her inner self and beauty were both made visible and kept well protected.

Artist B

- Initial conceptual ideas: hexagonal, medium weight, floating, multiple, honeycomb, shell textured.

- Drawing process: Artist B made an extensive exploration of her beehive concept through photocopy formats, mixed media and monoprints. This helped her to clarify her preferred colour scheme for the sculpture and to arrive at a multicell composition.

Sculptural construction process

Three different-sized hexagonal forms were cut from polystyrene and partly hollowed out to create cells (Figure 4.12). A deep-yellow satin was cut to shape and glued to cover the outside of the cells, which were then glued together. A stencilling and photocopy technique was used to create the patterning inside the cells. Letters were made from air-dried white clay to spell the words "hope, love, trust." "Hope" was placed in the largest of the cells, "trust" in the medium-sized cell and "love" in the smaller one (Figure 4.13). Care was taken in the arrangement of the letters in terms of sculptural composition. The compilation was then placed onto a large cotton wool pad which had been laid over foam board.

ART GROUPS 73

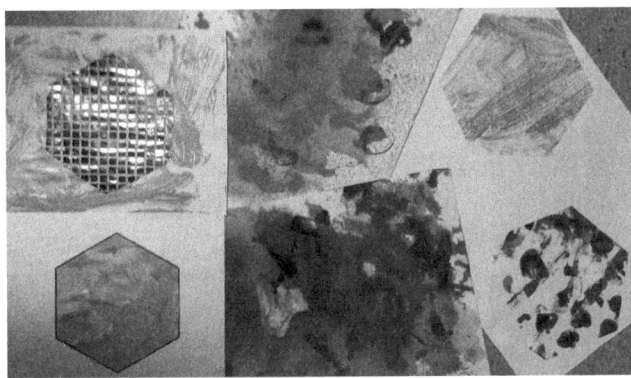

Figure 4.12 Artist B's testing of shape and media in collage (see insert for colour version)

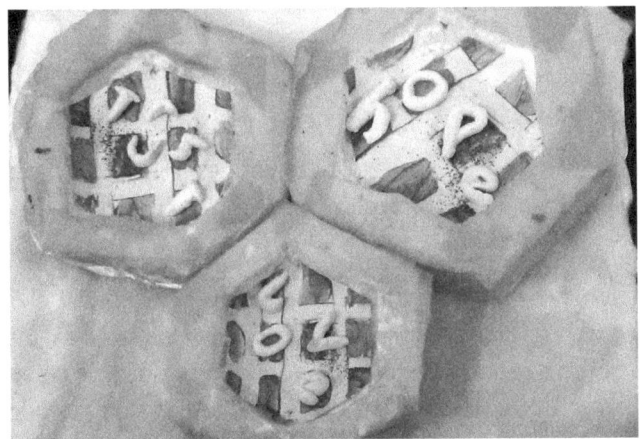

Figure 4.13 Artist B's sacred vessel marquette (see insert for colour version)

The following statement was given by Artist B:

> My sculpture is a beehive. It is precious to me because I have a friend who had beehives and he told me a lot about them. I would like to keep precious gems here. My beehive holds the words "love," "hope" and "trust" which are also precious, something to be guarded and taken care of.

> **Arts therapist's observations**
> The beehive was a place of activity, work and creation where there was the transformation of nectar into honey. This was reflective of Artist B's inner life, in which she was inspired, spiritually aware and seeking to reveal her individuality. The colours, material use and details conveyed the nature of the honeycomb and of those things the sculpture would come to signify. The key focus in her work became the preciousness of friendship and of having been recognised as worthy. Her friend had made an investment of sharing his work with her, which she treasured. Love, hope and trust were the glue that bound this friendship, qualities that held some fragility. Without them, friendships cannot survive.

Artist C

- Initial conceptual ideas: square, medium weight, floating, like a house with an open roof, incorporating wood.

- Drawing process: Artist C's exploration on paper was less extensive than those of Artists A and B. He had a clear vision from the start of what he wanted to create. In his drawing process he used a square to explore the shape and possible colour, which he further extended in monoprints. He then integrated his monoprints into his sculpture, as shown in Figure 4.14.

Sculptural construction process

A square box with a fitted lid was utilised as a found object to begin the sculptural construction. Monoprints that had been made in the drawing process were cut to shape to cover the container and glued into place. The inside of the box was lined with vertical wooden ice cream sticks. Artist C then layered ice cream sticks in a stack at the bottom of the box, which appeared random but was carefully composed and glued. The lid was covered with aqua-coloured satin fabric, hinged and then propped up with a wooden skewer.

Figure 4.14 Artist C's sacred vessel marquette

The following statement was given by Artist C:

> My sculpture is a square vessel that is like a house opening at the roof. The square shape connects me with my Taiwanese culture, which is very important to me. The vessel contains the potential of my goals expressed in the way I arranged the wood at the bottom, and the print on the outside displays my hopes for the future.

Arts therapist's observations

The square shape referenced Artist C's Taiwanese culture as the foundation of his identity. In his religion, Christianity, the human body has been referred to as "the temple of the soul" and the sturdiness of the box provided this connotation. The monoprints were a display of the inner reality externalised. The monoprint process had externalised the colours of the inner self in such a way that Artist C was greatly pleased by them, hence their inclusion on the outside surface of the sculpture. On the inside was a fence lining made of wood, and on the floor were those things that are still under construction through the process of self-awareness, goal setting, art focuses and manifestation into lifestyle. The viewer was invited to celebrate his identity and see what was inside the box.

Summary

The approaches were driven by therapeutic inquiry into archetypal spiritual notions of sacredness, preciousness and protection, while drawing upon the knowledge and conventions of contemporary fine art to provide a cultural basis. This resulted in sculptures that might have been found in a first-year art-degree programme. In addition to the therapeutic focus and archetypal engagement which took place, there were benefits of artmaking within the communal environment. Knill (2017b) has stated:

> communal art-making is…a learning experience which provides an individual, as well as a social, enabling and a situational coping. The effect of this experience is cognitive and physical. We can observe it in the change of emotion, mood and tone of the participants…the coping experience in the communal learning process of community art confronts the beliefs within the scope of: "We are not able to accomplish anything." (p.216)
>
> The communal artwork can touch or move the community members…the art-work makes sense in its beauty… It can be remembered as a touching, moving, regenerating, nourishing experience—a kind of "soul food." (p.217)

Members of the wider community of the organisation were invited to meet with the artists and enjoy the collection of fine art that had been produced. Both the works on paper and the sacred-vessel sculptures were displayed along with the artist's photographs, profiles and statements. People who attended had a chance to learn more about the lives, abilities and challenges of being an artist with a disability. There was a celebration of being able to accomplish great things, of having produced art capable of captivating and inspiring others who did not live with a disability. The sacred vessels stood in their own right, with their own stories to tell, and connected on an archetypal level with a receptive audience. The event itself became "a touching, moving, regenerating, nourishing experience—a kind of 'soul food'" which would remain memorable for the artists and the audience.

Conclusion

Three group art therapy journeys began in different ways and took different courses and foci. With technical assistance, participants were able to conceptualise and develop their personalised artworks through a series of stages to create an object of aesthetic significance. Each process engaged the archetypal approach, which led to transformational engagement within the imaginal realm and effected therapeutic outcomes relevant to individualised needs and goals.

CHAPTER 5

Environmental Sculpture

Keywords: archetypal shapes, chronology, heart energy, trauma, embodiment, natural objects

Environmental sculptors established conventions in fine art through working with found objects from nature to create visual interventions within landscapes, which invited the viewer to see nature in a new way. Within the environmental art movement, collections from nature were composed as installations within gallery spaces, and photographs of sculptures within nature environments became a form of secondary artwork (Goldsworthy 1990; Hill 1997).

For the client group with physical difficulties, opportunities to interact within and with the natural world were limited, so a special project was designed to allow them to work in natural locations. The aims were to use some of the ideas from environmental sculpture, to allow the participants to enjoy the freedom of being in the natural environment while creating art and to allow for the possibility of nature working a beneficial effect for the group members (Evans 2015; Roberts 2017; Whitaker 2017). Participants could establish connections with nature while also working with archetypal symbolism within the practices outlined by Jungian psychologists Arrien (1992) and Estes (1992).

Processes also involved the use of drawing and painting, which further consolidated self-reflection, integration and therapeutic outcomes. Environmental sculpture was demonstrated as providing benefits for people with physical disabilities within a multimodal arts therapy process. The approaches were further extended to accommodate other client groups with a focus on recovery from trauma.

The benefits and scope of using environmental media

Environmental sculptors have used collections from nature to create artworks which have often involved the circle or other geometric shapes and forms. In addition to the conservation messages that the artworks represented, the act of acquiring organic media brought the artists into multisensory communion with nature, in which there were therapeutic benefits. This knowledge formed the basis of an inquiry into how environmental art approaches might be incorporated into an arts therapeutic context.

In recent psychology research, Fabjanski and Brymer (2017) found that immersion in nature promoted increased "eudemonic [or eudaimonic] wellbeing and hedonic tone" (p.2). Ryan and Deci (2001) defined "eudaimonic" as being the degree of alignment with one's "daimon or true self" (p.146), and "hedonic" as the level of pleasure on a "pleasure/pain continuum" (p.144). "Nature based experiences might present a unique route to lasting and meaningful wellbeing outcomes" (Fabjanski and Brymer 2017, p.2). Activities in nature were found to have brought about enhanced "cognitive performance, social behaviour and affect," helped to reduce anxiety and lowered the "risks of mental health issues" (p.2).

Within an arts therapy context, Evans (2015) described how she made environmental artworks as an intervention for her own wellbeing, commenting on the rich sensory experience that took place. She stated that "a strong sense-memory remains: the smell of tree-ripened quinces, the hollow ring of bleached sheep bones touching each other, the weight of volcanic rock, the fragility of poppy petals, black flax seed slippery to the touch" (p.80). For Evans the use of the environment and organic media offered full engagement of the senses, increased enjoyment within the present moment and promoted artistic personalisation of nature beyond that of previously recognised art methodologies. It could stimulate a different kind of creative and therapeutic response which involved attuning with the natural world.

Working in nature provided the opportunity for people who had disabilities to strengthen their connection with nature while exploring their own life journeys through archetypal approaches that were creative and therapeutically dynamic. These approaches could also be applied with people who were fully able-bodied and had health and wellbeing goals.

The Intervention in Nature process

The Intervention in Nature process utilised Arrien's (1992) five archetypal shapes as a containment for environmental sculpture creations and cultivated social connection through the group process. Arrien identified that five geometric shapes appeared in the art of all cultures, with people in different cultures giving similar meaning to these shapes (p.12):

Circle (wholeness)

Square (stability)

Triangle (goals and dreams)

Cross (relationships)

Spiral (growth)

Arrien further stated that the meaning attributed to each shape stands for a process in human growth and that the shape carries this within itself (p.12).

In the context of arts therapy, an intuitive approach was favoured which gave a point of entry into the process based on personal choice, with a belief that the creative process would lead into phenomenological dimensions of healing and be extended through the unconscious. Participants were provided with an overview of Arrien's theories for each of the five shapes and invited to choose the one that most resonated. They then worked in pairs to create an environmental artwork which combined both of their chosen shapes, which may have been different (Figure 5.1) or the same (Figure 5.2). They were offered the opportunity to move collaboratively beyond the initial shapes, whereby a metamorphosis through a range of shapes could take place, thus potentially extending therapeutic benefits. Benefits took place on multiple levels which enhanced holistic wellbeing and creativity.

Figure 5.1 Pairs sculpture using adjoined spiral shapes

Figure 5.2 Sculpture within features of environment, and painting from photograph (see insert for colour version)

Participants identified their primary reasons for attending arts therapy groups and workshops in the community. These reasons were categorised as follows:

- Mental health and holistic wellbeing
    - To overcome depression and other mental health symptoms
    - To promote recovery from physical health concerns
    - To experience rejuvenation
    - To experience mindfulness
- Catalyse changes
    - To overcome addictions such as alcohol overuse or lack of dietary control
    - To overcome creative inertia

- Social
    - To meet new people
    - To encounter social connectedness
    - To experience a positive social environment
    - To be with other creative or like-minded people
- Knowledge/skills
    - To learn new arts techniques
    - To extend knowledge and skills within the arts therapies
    - To make new self-discoveries
- Creativity
    - To be creatively stimulated
    - To find new inspiration and creative direction
    - To establish new goals for the future

The Arts Therapy 5-Pt Star model (see Chapter 2) was used to ensure that diverse therapeutic and educational goals of participants were met through providing a focus for both the development of interventions and the way in which sessions were structured. In developing the Intervention in Nature process, the five domains of the model were considered: self-reflection; transformational engagement; relationships; aesthetic skills; and lifestyle development. This also maximised the holistic benefits of participating in the process.

The use of the Arrien archetypal symbols targeted transformational engagement and self-reflection while also bringing containment to the aesthetic. Changes which occurred on an internal level through transformational engagement could affect improvements in relationships and lead to lifestyle changes. The relationship domain was targeted through the group's process of positive social experiences, and in the final transitional reflection, the question was posed of what benefits there might be from the workshop in terms of lifestyle.

Case study: Jack's multimedia environmental sculpture process

Jack attended a community-based arts therapy three-day workshop which focused on enhancing wellbeing and creativity. He had previously experienced mental health challenges and was interested in how arts processes could provide therapeutic benefits; however, his main reason for attending was "to be a part of the group." The group met up in an art room and after introductions to each other and the programme overview, environmental sculpture was introduced as the first art process.

When asked to pair up, Jack chose to work with a man whom he already knew and who had come to the group with similar interests. Jack had chosen the cross, while his partner had chosen the circle, and once out in the natural environment, they selected items from the resources provided which had been collected from the seaside. The environment was one with which he was familiar, a coastal farm and park reserve near his home which he had previously used for recreational walks. The two men wandered through the fields to collect additional natural materials and find a suitable site for their sculpture. Eventually they arrived at a circle of stones embedded on uneven, grassy ground. They decided to use the stone circle as a basis of their artwork and to integrate their archetypal symbols there. Jack placed his cross within the circle using a piece of driftwood and shells.

During their search for suitable resources, they had found a triangular piece of tyre rubber, which had appealed to them as a manufactured element. The triangle symbol became central to the artwork, which had then morphed into a mandala with a star of shells and a floral tribute.

At the next stage, they joined the bigger group for presentations in pairs. There was a sense of artistic triumph and celebration in talking about their joint creative journey. The group members were amused by their imaginative and witty use of resources. Their sculptures had been photographed and then ceremoniously left behind as an environmental tribute. Jack had also enjoyed the presentations of creations by the other pairs. He returned to the art room for the next stage of the workshop feeling both energised and relaxed. There was a sense that everyone had connected, and this met some of the hopes he had held in attending.

The next two days mostly involved drawing and painting with a focus on the imaginal realm and self-exploration. On the third day, there was the suggestion of making a symbolic painting on canvas that would encapsulate the arts therapy experience of the entire weekend. Jack decided he would use the photograph from his environmental sculpture and engage with this further. His painting took on even stronger dimensions of mandala with greater geometry and regularity coming into the composition. In Jungian Sandplay Therapy the spontaneous appearance of a mandala using symbols can denote the completion of a process and some integration (Turner 2017; Weinrib 2004; Kalff 2003). Jack spontaneously chose this as a means of consolidation, closure and fluidity in self-expression.

McNiff (2004) observed that, "Different materials and environments will elicit creative expressions in keeping with their structures" (p.20). Both the sculpture in the environment and photographic representation were fixed images (see Figure 5.2). The completed symbol was "brought home" in terms of soul in the form of free-flowing paint. The painting was then hung in pride of place in Jack's dwellings as a lasting tribute to the event. It has stood as a vibrant representation of himself and has accompanied the successful life journey that he has since made.

In the construction of their sculpture some pairs stayed with their two chosen archetypal shapes, while for others a metamorphosis took place whereby further shapes from the five domains became incorporated, as in the case of Jack and his partner. Processes took place spontaneously and collaboratively without the need for discussion. The belief was held that whatever direction the artworks took, they would lead to transformational outcomes through unconscious processes. "Healing energies will always find their way to areas of need within a person or group… Discoveries, insights and changes occur through the 'complex' of imagination that integrates and sometimes makes use of unlikely sources" (McNiff 2017, p.27).

Participants reported that the process facilitated benefits on a holistic level which included invigoration, self-reflection, social connection, improved emotional wellbeing, and rejuvenation. They reported moving toward new ideas and directions both artistically and in life.

Time-Life-Lines

The concept of Time-Life-Lines was developed in practice as an accessible process for people with physical disabilities and an opportunity to target some specific needs of clients within the rehabilitation service setting. The framework synthesised two different timeline concepts which had been a part of psychology practices (Estes 1992; Cameron 1997) and used an art therapy lens to develop a process which drew upon the natural environmental as a source of media (Evans 2015). The involvement with natural objects offered a multisensory experience and the benefits of nature offered connection and attuning (Fabjanski and Brymer 2017).

Specific needs that were targeted were those associated with being able to put life events into context, which provided an opportunity to see and appreciate a bigger perspective. It was therapeutically significant to have defining events, painful and positive, acknowledged and appreciated. Most participants had encountered traumatic events through the course of their lives, and the framework provided an opportunity to locate the trauma within "the past…[securing] the context of the event in time and space" (Rothschild 2000, p.155). It offered a form of public recognition that was akin to "a positive homecoming" (Lubin and Johnson 2008, p.93), which was facilitating of new beginnings toward the future. In this approach, participants could externalise their life journeys in a linear way and as a significant whole. This created visibility for people who had felt marginalised through the suggestion that their life stories held little significance for the wider society. It provided a means of recognition and integration toward events that had been important that had gone unrecognised.

Organic objects collected from nature were used to illustrate the timeline through their different shapes, textures, colours and structures, which provided the metaphoric element and brought the stories to life symbolically. The sensory benefits of being in touch with nature enhanced the therapeutic process. "The natural world has the ability to effortlessly hold our attention (i.e., soft fascination) and restore our cognitive resources" (Fabjanski and Brymer 2017, p.2). Drawing and painting were utilised at different stages of the process, and Arrien's (2002) geometric shapes were introduced as a part of a sculptural integrative end process.

Development of the framework

In the development of the timeline aspect of the framework, Estes (1992, pp.364–376) offered a process which she had termed *descansos*, the Spanish word for rest or resting place. In her approach you mark out the "roads not taken, paths that were cut off, ambushes, betrayals and death" (p.365) using the symbol of crosses along a timeline. The cross was used as a metaphor in the timeline to anchor those things which had been losses, which had led to a sense of liberation and the integration of unresolved anger and grief.

Cameron (1997, pp.44–57) also presented a useful approach in "the narrative timeline" which was concerned with the authenticity of the stories, and particularly those which formed the basis of personal identity. She made the distinction between those we carry which have been externally imposed and those which are seen through the joy and warmth of our own lens. "Stories that we *choose* to tell and cherish about ourselves are the true stories, the road map to the real, lantern-hearted self" (p.46).

Through conceptually integrating the approaches of both Estes and Cameron, the Time-Life-Lines framework invited a balanced view toward the losses and triumphs of a person's life. These were recognised as having been the defining moments in becoming the person we had each become and points worthy of celebration. There was an honouring of the struggles and pains alongside gifts and life-giving interventions. It was important to provide this balance of "negative" with "positive" for people who had suffered trauma and day-to-day struggles through living with a disability. There was the opportunity to acknowledge and share traumatic and difficult events while also recognising the landmarks of achievements and growth. Reframing unresolved events within a bigger picture of life journeys had honoured the whole person with their strengths and talents. This engendered hope for the future.

Case study: Group journey through Time-Life-Lines

Step 1

A timeline was drawn out by marking five- or ten-year intervals (depending on the person's age) on a large sheet of paper, with a generous expanse toward the future. Common life themes, such as hospital encounters, schooling, birthday celebrations, travel and milestone achievements, were explored. This began the process of recalling and recording the chronologies. Staff took the role of scribe for remembered events. There was a process of patient questioning and answering to fully capture the chronologies of events. This continued until the person was satisfied with the accuracy of the story.

There were surprises in some of the timelines. A man wanted to acknowledge that his family had celebrated every birthday since he was six years old, each one being memorable (see Figure 5.5). Despite her disabilities, a woman who had attended a mainstream school had achieved sports awards. A European man had a second home on the Pacific island of Fiji through his adopted sister who was born there. There were events that had caused deep sadness such as the death of a parent or the death of a child. Everyone in the group had experienced being in hospital for different kinds of medical interventions and illnesses. All knew what it was like to struggle and to triumph.

Step 2
Resources from nature were presented and the process of using natural objects as metaphor was explained. The participants chose from the existing coastal collections and were assisted to gather additional materials from the gardens surrounding the building. The experience of noticing what nature held in an urban setting and finding items that resonated with each participant brought nature into close focus. A spikey ball, a smooth flat leaf, jagged rock, polished stone, forked stick; items collected became treasured elements toward metaphor and artmaking.

Step 3
One by one, natural objects were placed along the timeline as the visual descriptors of how the identified events had been experienced. The items communicated effectively while also inviting further questioning and recognition of how the events had been for the person. For example, "You chose a big, rough-looking rock for that. Does that mean it was quite a hard time for you?" "That dried flower looks like a star ball. Is that a celebration or does it mean something else?" Selected natural objects were then colour enhanced using a dying process.

Step 4
Timelines were photographed so that they could be reconstructed or the photograph could serve as a point of reference.

Step 5
Participants explored selected events from their timelines through paintings (Figure 5.3), which were shared as a part of the group process. In terms of articulating the events in paint media, the colour of the paper chosen as a background was a significant beginning point. Providing a diverse range of colour options brought in contrasts, highlights and signified the rich tapestry of a person's life.

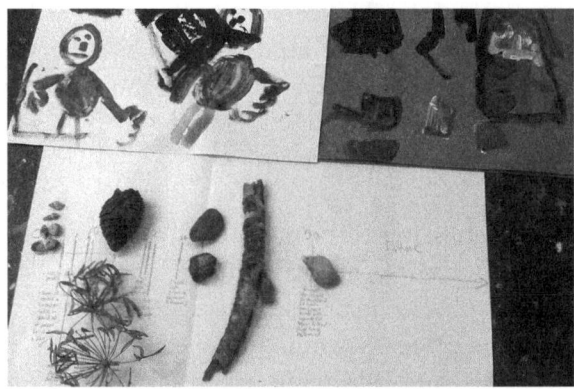

Figure 5.3 Timeline chronology and nature objects; paintings of selected events

Step 6
A range of dye baths suitable for organic materials were created in red, orange, gold, lime green, jade green, azure, blue and purple. Participants enhanced some of their selected objects using the dye baths. Selected objects were also decorated using paint.

Step 7
Containers were chosen or made in which a sculptural monument was constructed using air-dried clay and objects from the timeline. Here the five archetypal shapes (Arrien 1992, p.12) were suggested in three-dimensional form, with other shapes also being offered as possibilities.

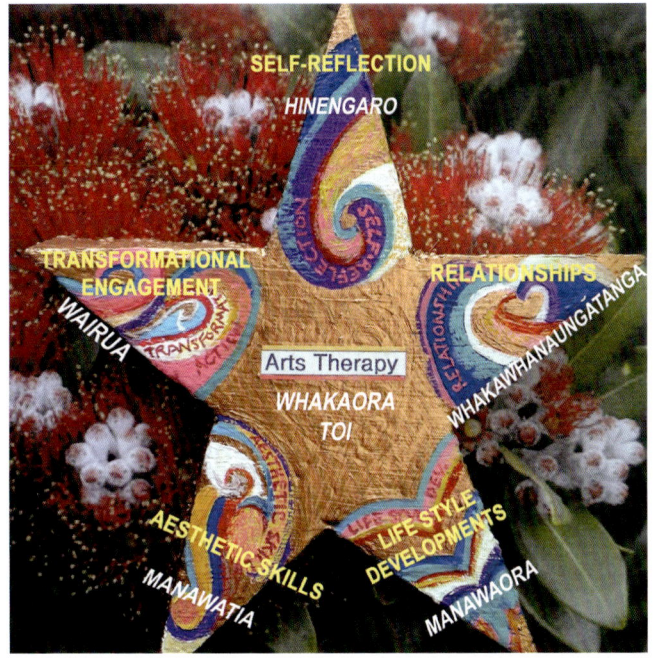

Figure 2.1 Arts Therapy 5-Pt Star Model in English and Māori

Figure 2.2 Arts Therapy 5-Pt Star domains

Figure 2.4 The participant (Andy) using a wheelchair tray for layout and reflection on symbols

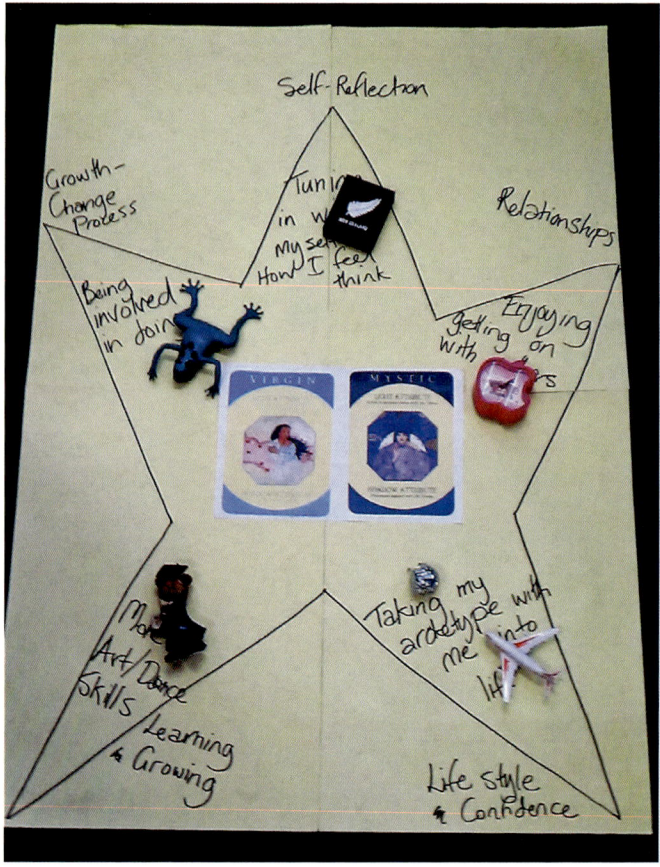

Figure 2.5 The dance arts group participant's (Andy's) symbols laid out in 5-Pt Star format

Figure 3.1 Example of a relationship map using name tags and symbols

Figure 3.2 A similar smaller-sized tribute being released into water

Figure 3.3 Completed fairy garden

Figure 3.5 Series of paintings "fairies in their garden"

Figure 4.7 Inside the treasure box was the photo of a chief navigating the seas

Figure 4.12 Artist B's testing of shape and media in collage

Figure 4.13 Artist B's sacred vessel marquette

Figure 5.2 Sculpture within features of environment, and painting from photograph

Figure 5.4 Tributary monuments which integrated nature objects from timeline

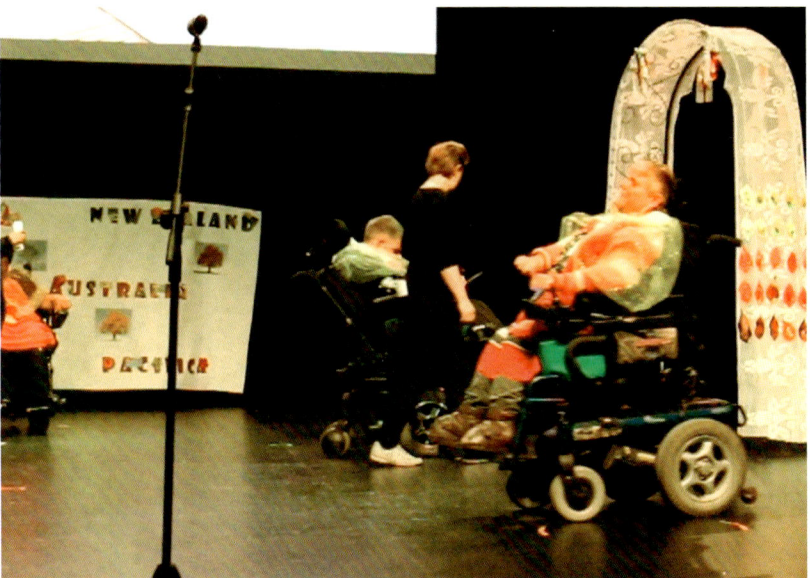

Figure 6.9 Embodying the role in dance 6

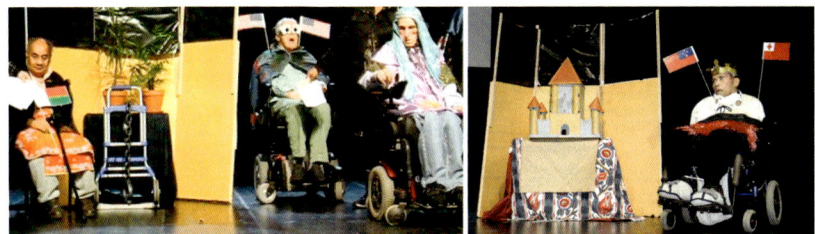

Figure 7.10 The actors in their public performance at InterACT Festival in Auckland

Figure 9.1 Holding the four archetypal elements

Step 8

Monuments were created as tributes to life journeys which included hopes for the future (Figures 5.4 and 5.5). Through this, events were visually and psychologically brought to a point of integration whereby the person's past, present and future stood as a consolidated whole, and on a visual level, artworks made a statement of passion, creativity, originality and aesthetic care. In the case of Figure 5.5, this sculpture became a part of a debut gallery exhibition of artworks by four painters. His monument, which had signified his life story using objects from the seaside, became the catalyst for paintings that further explored his life and connections with the sea. This led to the fulfillment of a vocational aspiration of becoming recognised as an artist.

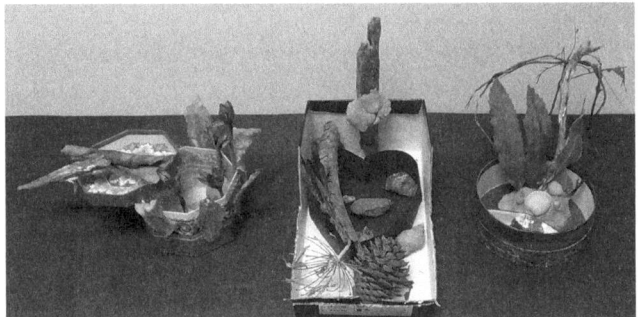

Figure 5.4 Tributary monuments which integrated nature objects from timeline (see insert for colour version)

Figure 5.5 "Colours of my life and the sea" including more than 20 birthday celebrations

Step 9
Participants were invited to talk about the process but found that difficult, so paint emerged as a preferred means of dialogue. Some group members were then able to articulate their thoughts vocally: "The painting at the end was really important, that's all I've got to say." "God be with you." "I'm not sure what it means, but I want to do it all over again straight away!" This came as a very fitting end to the group process.

Summary
As in the case of Jack in the Intervention in Nature process, the opportunity of creating a painted response to nature sculptures proved pivotal in terms of meaning making and integration. Being able to extend the process through a different art form to derive meaning was effective. Making a creative response came more naturally leading to poetic utterances; and in the case of people who were non-verbal, painting was the key mode of externalising thoughts. McNiff (2017) stated:

> The use of different art media enriches the ecology of imagination. We cultivate imagination by feeding it with possible resources, by deepening the mix of ingredients, and always trusting that this integrative intelligence will find its way to healing and re-constructive powers of the creative imagination. (p.30)

Being in nature and handling collected organic objects brought participants into the present moment where the focus was on being observant and using the senses. Working with archetypal symbolic shapes and approaches brought positive cognitive and creative challenges related to containment while at the same time providing connection with the unconscious mind, through which healing transformation could take place. The use of drawing and painting contributed in ways that were facilitating and integrative. A creative-therapies lens of multiarts modes was useful in maximising therapeutic outcomes.

Introduction of the labyrinth for diverse contexts: trauma

The process of Time-Life-Lines was further adapted to cater for diverse client groups including people with disabilities, where there was a focus on recovery from trauma. There was an extension into a further archetypal dimension into labyrinths with a focus on movement and enactment that addressed the role of embodiment in trauma. The approaches were provided in workshops for practitioners who were seeking experiences that could be applied with their own clients. Through working in different venues, there were nuances in processes which arrived at differences in outcomes through adapting approaches to suit the space.

In developing the new direction, there was consideration toward people who had experienced trauma and disabilities through earthquakes and other natural disasters, and the role that site played in recovery. There was a deep sense of connection between people and the places in which damage had occurred as part of their traumatic experience. There was the notion that this could be honoured as sacred ground through the therapeutic process. Labyrinths offered a means of presenting a timeline and supported the notion of ritual and sacred ground.

Labyrinths date back to Egyptian, Greek and Roman mythology. A few years previously, I had participated in a "walk-the-labyrinth" opportunity, which had been attributed to the early Christians. The unicursal Christian symbol had been drawn out on a large cloth which was travelling around the world. The layout was said to have been used at a time when Christian pilgrimage had become too dangerous, and the journey had then been made symbolically. The experience of walking across a sacred cloth with meditational intent had left a lasting impression in terms of embodiment. This seemed an appropriate archetypal connection when considering the role of embodiment and the disassociation in trauma (Rothschild 2000).

Research led to the discovery of a diverse range of unicursal patterns which were presented to inspire individual direction within a Time-Life-Line process. The underpinnings of Estes (1992) and Cameron (1997) were also presented, and then a meditational exercise followed in which visualisation of a personal labyrinth was encouraged through posing the question, "What shape is the route to your heart?"

Instructions for the process
The instructions were as follows:

1. What shape is the route to your heart?

2. You could use a shape that comes to mind or a straight line to create your Time-Life-Line. Draw this out on a large sheet of paper.

3. What are the significant events of your life as they reveal themselves to you today?

4. Write a quick chronology.

5. Use your labyrinth or linear shape to create a map of significant events by marking each onto your labyrinth or timeline, and then labelling each with the year and an associated word or phrase.

6. From the natural objects, find those that best symbolise the significant events that you have charted, that is, look at size, texture, colour, repetition, strength, function in nature and so forth. Place them on the appropriate points of your Time-Life-Line.

7. Walk or dance the shape of your Time-Life-Line, honouring the chosen objects which symbolise the significant events.

8. Take a moment to appreciate the journey that you have made.

9. Create a sculpture that encapsulates the wholeness of your journey and experience by using the natural object from your layout.

10. Add adornments that symbolise aspirations and goals for the future.

In addition to natural organic objects, there were collections that had been through a dyeing process to produce a range of subtle colour enhancements. There were also pieces of disused costume jewellery, beads, glass tablets, artificial flowers, pearls, feathers and other objects. Wire, string, air-dried clay and other agents were provided for the construction of the monuments.

The focus was on providing an experience to practitioners through an embodied process that they could then provide to their clients. A variety of music tracks provided an added creative stimulus and encouraged movement following their individual labyrinth path. A ritual or meditative gesture toward the monument was also encouraged as a means of completion.

In a smaller room, tables were positioned in a square or circle leaving a space in the middle of the room. The adornments were placed on the floor at the heart centre of the space. Movement took place in this central arena as a walk or dance along the labyrinth pathway to selecting adornments at the symbolic heart centre. The movement aspect became a taster rather than a full exploration; however, there were playful dance moves and pathway shapes created as a symbolic token of walking the labyrinth. Feedback suggested that the overall process had provided a valuable educational experience and that the framework could be readily utilised in practice.

Where the room was larger, additional resources, such as scarves and percussion instruments, could be made available for use. This meant that there was a greater opportunity to explore the notion of embodiment and for experimentation with expressive movement to take place within a chosen area of the room. For some practitioners, the multimodal depth exploration proved a strong catalyst in terms of their own process, and the journey was affirmed as bringing a powerful connection with heart energy, leading to significant personal growth and greater wellbeing.

In a context specific to a group of people who have physical disabilities, it is suggested that they would be able to paint their labyrinth and then the path could be embodied through wheelchair movement or dance. The approach of creating a central space with adornments at the heart centre would be useful whereby each participant could be witnessed by the group in their movement pathway. The other steps in the process could be carried out as took place in the earlier Time-Life-Lines intervention.

Conclusion

Environmental sculpture in multimodal arts therapy combined the benefits of working with natural objects with the archetypal frameworks. Intervention in Nature utilised Arrien's (2002) five symbolic shapes to create artworks within nature environments, and where therapeutic benefits were extended through other art media. Time-Life-Lines, which utilised the approaches of Estes (1992) and Cameron (1997), was developed to provide an accessible process for people with disabilities which directly targeted their needs. A further archetypal development was the use of a labyrinth in which movement and embodiment were components. Each of the approaches have demonstrated significant therapeutic outcomes and can be made accessible for people who have physical disabilities.

CHAPTER 6

Expressive Dance Movement

Keywords: mythology, seasons, animus, collectivism, choreography, embodiment, performance, mobility goals

Dance arts developed within the parameters of a particular space, where the approaches used came about in response to the interests, and the abilities and disabilities, of a particular client group. Group interests included the opportunity to perform on stage at InterACT Festival, a three-day annual event which showcased the artistic abilities of people who had disabilities. Archetypes provided a key dimension of therapeutic encounter through the course of weekly or fortnightly group sessions, which culminated in performance pieces. The two group studies recounted here, "Legends of Maui" and "Around the World Through the Seasons," provide a contrast in how using archetypes led to positive therapeutic and performance outcomes.

Development of dance arts in a multidisciplinary team context

Dance arts was a multimodal group forum which was developed within the rehabilitation service, where physiotherapy was prioritised through funding contracts. The benefits of music and movement were recognised within the multidisciplinary setting and the notion that dance arts could support physical mobility goals gave greater impetus toward development and inclusion. The dance arts framework evolved through client-led approaches which explored expressive movement and choreography in conjunction with artmaking. Therapeutic benefits took place on multiple levels through physical and emotional responses to music, archetypal engagement, dramatic enactment, artmaking and social interaction.

Lewis (1996) stated that dance therapy includes "all forms of traditional and non-traditional performance art, ethnographic ritual dance, folk, and societal dance. But it also includes the dance of everyday gesture and…[of] relationships" (pp.96–97). Dance processes drew upon traditional forms in conjunction with expressive dance movement (Halprin and Weller 2003).

Archetypes provided a key dimension of therapeutic encounter through symbolism, toward improved emotional and psychological wellbeing, and as the basis of embodied characterisation, which was significant in circumstances where movement was restricted through physical disabilities. Outcomes were demonstrated to be positive toward overall therapy goals through the Arts Therapy 5-Pt Star Assessment, which provided qualitative and quantitative evaluation of progress for individuals within groups (Gordon-Flower 2014b, pp.104–119).

The physiotherapy gym space allowed a maximum of six people in wheelchairs, with additional people not in wheelchairs, to participate and assist. The involvement of interns, volunteers or support staff made dance possible, as some people who used manual chairs relied on full assistance, and others required some support with driving their motorised chairs within the choreography. Some participants who did not use wheelchairs also needed assistance because of blindness, intellectual disability, social anxiety, autism or through having an unsteady gait when walking and dancing.

Sessions were one-and-a-half hours in duration and structured to include warm-ups and a selection of activities from the group choreographic and artmaking processes as outlined below.

Warm-ups in response to music
Tuning in with oneself
Participants were asked to tune in to their current feelings and start to express them in some way through movement, including moving on the spot and around the space, and to discover their favoured movement expression. It was suggested that feelings could be expressed and/or transformed through engaging with the music and dance movement.

Tuning in with others
Participants were asked to find a movement that they enjoyed, and an opportunity was provided for each person to lead the group, who mirrored the movement. They were asked to create a dance together in pairs and then sometimes in threes. Each person was asked to take a turn in utilising the large central floor space, to create a solo dance in response to a soundtrack, which the group witnessed and appreciated.

Developing choreographed movement for stage performance
Working with an archetypal focus
Participants developed a character for longer-term exploration within the group, and then chose music and symbols to support embodiment of the character.

Working with a choreography approach
Each participant led a dance in character whereby the other dancers used the same choreographed movements or other movements that supported the lead. This created a sequence of dances which encapsulated each person's character and offered a variety of choreographed movements within a theme.

Making artworks
Responding to movement using painting and reflecting on experiences
Participants were asked to reflect on how they had experienced themselves in the dance and how they felt in expressing their character, or to express their feelings in the current moment.

Exploring symbols of identity within a theme through mixed media
Participants were asked to consider images and colours that best represented their character and dance story.

Creating props and costumes to express dance character
Dancers researched and designed costumes utilising preferred materials and incorporating chosen colours and symbols that reflected characterisation.

The combining of expressive dance movement with multimodal media offered greater opportunities for engagement and transformation through creative play (Gordon-Flower 2014b; Halprin and Weller 2003).

In working with archetypal themes, Ellis (2001) stated:

> The *symbolic realm* is a place of play and creativity, where material is generally not known at a conscious level… The movement metaphor affords symbolic meaning that is not necessarily overtly known… The dance/movement therapist may extrapolate meaning or hypotheses… from the movement metaphor to bring themes not actively known to the client to their attention. (p.182)

The archetypal themes of Maui in Māori mythology, and the theme of the seasons, came about through the process of the "symbolic and knowing realms…and intuitive response to metaphorical material, which informs an intervention without reaching a place of [fully] conscious attention" (Ellis 2001, p.182). The ideas were presented as possibilities and resonated with the group members as areas of interest. Throughout the course of engagement in the processes, connections emerged between the therapeutic needs of group members and the benefits of the theme foci as interventions.

The notion of embodying an archetypal role was a strong component of the approaches used, in lieu of freedom of physical movement. "Embodiment is an existential condition in which the body is the subjective source or intersubjective ground of experience" (Csordas 1999, p.143). "In the embodied arts therapies of dance and drama" transformation takes place in the "imaginal realm" (Lewis 1996, p.98). "As children, most individuals have engaged in fantasy and pretended to be any number of characters" with the knowledge that the roles were not real. This involved "being these characters with every inch of their bodies, so that their movements emerged naturally from this imaginal core…playing [in role] has a profound effect in shaping the individuals' adaptation to life" (Lewis 1996, p.98).

This kind of play had not necessarily been available for people who had disabilities in childhood; however, the participants demonstrated the ability to easily take on roles.

Embodiment was evident in body language including posture, facial expressions, angle of the head, eye contact and non-verbal social engagement, and the carrying out of actions spontaneously and through choreographed movements. Even for those who had minimal independent body movement, changes in the body language toward embodiment of roles could be recognised. Motorised wheelchairs served as an extension of the body and could form part of embodied movement expression. They could also hinder expression when challenges were encountered in control of speed and direction, in which case assistance was required in order for the person to hold an embodied role.

The goal of public performance was a strong motivation for attendance at weekly or fortnightly sessions. The journey toward performance was recognised as providing the key therapeutic benefits alongside a transformational aspect to being on stage and being recognised as having the ability to perform. There was correlation with Theatre of Witness productions (Sepinuck 2013), where being on stage brought visibility and metaphorically gave "a voice to those who have been marginalized, forgotten, or invisible to larger society" (p.14). The public audiences who bore witness and responded to the dancers in their archetypal roles and artistic strengths also had a key role in the therapeutic aspects. The dancers were empowered with greater confidence and gained a sense of having connected and been appreciated, which enhanced their self-esteem. There was a sense that the dancers had enriched the lives of the audience through their interpretation of the archetypes and their artistic contribution, which motivated the participants to seek further opportunities to participate, with further benefits.

Case study: Legends of Maui

The "Legends of Maui" from Māori mythology were chosen as a dance arts theme through which archetypal engagement, characterisation, movement and artmaking took place. Engagement with Māori legends of origin, creation and hero myth, of which Maui stories were a part, has been recognised as a key aspect in the ongoing construction of collective Māori identity (Majid 2010, p.13). Through participating in Māori mythology, there was an alignment with the bicultural interests of *Aotearoa*/New Zealand nationhood. At the same time, the stories involved universal themes and qualities.

There were variations of the Maui stories found in other Pacific cultures and also different versions within Māori culture. The aspects of the stories that the group became interested in were as follows:

Maui was a demigod who was premature at birth and not expected to survive. His mother wrapped him in a knot of her hair and released him to the ocean. There he was rescued by Tangaroa, god of the sea, and grew up to have supernatural powers. He was the youngest of five brothers and when he sought out his family as an adult, his mother was initially in disbelief that he was her son. The relationship that developed with his brothers was one of being left out and of being the subject of jealousy. Only when he hid on their fishing boat was he able to accompany them on a fishing trip. He then began to demonstrate his superhuman powers, including fishing up an extra-large haul of fish and then pulling up the North Island of *Aotearoa* (New Zealand) from out of the sea. His brothers were then willing to help him, and together they performed the feat of capturing the sun to slow down its path across the sky, thus creating longer days.

Two groups each of five people worked with the same theme but developed different parts of the story through their individual and group interests. They then became one large group of ten to perform as the whole cast on stage. The dancers could take on any role from the stories that resonated with them, and could create additional roles. In the larger group, there were two Maui characters: one of Maui's brothers had acquired a wife, and there was a *taniwha*, a mystical water creature which had arrived unexpectedly. Two of the women chose to take on roles of Maui's brothers, and another Tangaroa, god of the sea. In choosing male roles, the required tasks and actions had resonated strongly with the women. At the same time, there was an opportunity to explore gender and/or aspects of animus in the positive, which included "enterprising spirit, courage, truthfulness" and spirituality (Jung 1964, pp.194–195).

Group 1: Roles
The roles of group 1 were as follows:

- Mother of Maui, Taranga
- Maui in three different tasks
- *Taniwha*, mystical water creature
- Brother of Maui who helps to catch the sun
- Brother of Maui who catches a fish to feed his family

Group 1: Dancing of role developments

The dancing of the role developments of group 1 went as follows:

1. Taranga prepares to put baby Maui in the water.

   Taranga dances a sad lament as she holds her baby in her arms cradled in a little boat made of her hair and prepares to release him into the sea.

   The group support her dance using similar movements from behind her.

2. Taranga releases her baby into the water and moves away.

   The whole group (including Taranga) moves into a tight circle formation and then moves out to form a larger circle.

3. Maui performs a sequence.

   Maui meets his mother, Taranga, and they dance around each other.

   He begins fishing and pulls up a *taniwha*, who makes his own dance.

   He then fishes up *Te Ikaroa a Maui*, the North Island, a shape made through the formation of the group.

4. The brother is catching the sun with *harakeke* ropes (danced by a woman).

   The brother has big *harakeke* flax ropes which he throws up and uses to help pull the sun down.

   The group dance behind her following her lead of movements.

5. The brother is fishing (danced by a woman).

   The brother dances with his fishing line to catch the fish for his *whanau* (family). The remaining group dance behind her following her lead of movements.

The personal history of participants in group 1, relevant to roles, is given in Table 6.1.

Table 6.1 Personal history of participants relevant to roles (group 1)

Character	Therapeutic interests of dancer	Benefits
Taranga, mother of Maui	She was born prematurely and not expected to survive. She was still seeking a resolution to grief that had come about through separation from her mother.	She was able to experience the role of a mother who had to let go of her child, while also experiencing the support of the group.
Maui in three different tasks	He was striving to achieve lofty and worthwhile goals in several domains including the arts, advocacy and employment.	He was able to experience himself as empowered and potent in his abilities, which was an encouragement toward his life goals.
Taniwha, mystical water creature	He found an opportunity to express his own Māori cultural identity in a playful way that could bring joy.	There were limited opportunities for him to engage in Māori cultural concepts and he was able to express his identity and personality in a way that was empowering and creative.
Brother of Maui who helps to catch the sun (danced by a woman)	She had been disconnected from her family at birth and institutionalised, which had added to her sense of marginalisation and alienation from the rest of society.	Being a part of a family and able to assist with an important task was highly significant.
Brother of Maui who catches a fish to feed his family (danced by a woman)	She had immigrated to New Zealand from one of the Pacific Islands where fishing had been a part of the lifestyle.	She was able to express an aspect of her cultural heritage and the environment in which she grew up. This was significant to retaining her personal and cultural identity.

Group 2: Roles

The roles of group 2 were as follows:

- Tangaroa, god of the sea
- Maui, who pulls up *Te Ikaroa a Maui*, the North Island

- Brother of Maui who helps to catch the sun
- Wife who helps her husband with the task of catching the sun
- Brother who catches a good haul of fish

Group 2: Dancing of role developments

The dancing of the role developments of group 2 went as follows:

1. Tangaroa, god of the sea, finds Maui and rescues him, transforming him.

   Maui is completely covered over with a cloth like a rock in the water.

   Tangaroa dances around him bestowing him with magical powers and then unveils him.

   This reveals Maui, the grown-up man who dances around and tests his powers.

2. The brother and his wife catch the sun together.

   The brother and his wife both hold *harakeke* (flax) ropes that reach all the way to the sun which they pull on to drag the sun down.

   The group moves behind them following their movements.

3. The brother pulls up lots of fish onto the boat for his *whanau* (family).

   The brother uses his wheelchair tilt as he fishes, his boat bobbing up and down on the sea with the weight of the haul he is pulling in.

   The group mirror his moves showing the opposite: when he goes up, they go down and so forth.

4. Maui has a tug of war pulling up *Te Ikaroa a Maui*, the North Island.

   There is a great tug of war between Maui and the remaining group who form *Te Ikaroa a Maui*.

Movement of the group is forward and then backward a little, forward some more and then backward a little, until he has dragged them across the stage.

Maui, who is facing them, moves forward and backward in connection with them.

The stories developed by the dancers within the two groups, the characterisation and the music selection, brought strong motivation toward movement which included the performance of physical acts in reaching for the sun, fishing in the sea and taking part in a tug of war. These acts supported the physiotherapy goals of extending physical agility and range of movement.

The personal history of participants in group 2, relevant to roles, is given in Table 6.2.

Table 6.2 Personal history of participants relevant to roles (group 2)

Character	Therapeutic interests of dancer	Benefits
Tangaroa, god of the sea	She often felt disempowered, which led to conflict.	She gained the experience of what it was like to hold power in a positive way and to empower someone else's potential.
Maui who pulls up Te Ikaroa a Maui, the North Island	He had strong leadership potential which had not found a rightful place in a career role.	He was able to work with a role within the dance where his actions led and influenced the whole group.
Brother of Maui who helps to catch the sun	He was interested in being in a loving partnership relationship with a significant other.	He was able to experience being supported by a partner and doing an important task together.
Wife who helps her husband with the task of catching the sun	She was interested in being in a loving partnership relationship with a significant other.	She was able to experience what it was like to have an equal role alongside a partner in performing an important task.
Brother of Maui who catches a large haul of fish	He had a fatherly quality that did not find many opportunities for expression.	He was able to express his benevolence and take care of a family group through providing enough fish to feed his family and the community.

Through engaging with the archetypal story in mythology, there were underlying themes which were common to a collective. These themes included having a difficult birth, being abandoned, being rescued, being excluded, undergoing a transformation and discovering hidden abilities. These themes acted to the therapeutic benefit of the group as a whole. The dancers were also able to create unique roles which allowed them to experiment with areas of their own personal development and healing.

Therapeutic progress through the archetypal stories

Each of the dancers developed a personalised character from the mythological archetypes which, with their therapeutic interests and needs, provided an opportunity to experience life roles, some of which were outside the scope of what was possible in their everyday lives.

Each of the dancers found expression for their personal therapeutic interests through working with the archetypal stories. Each person took a lead role in the dance with the group choreography providing support for their character role and appointed tasks. The notion of group support was consistent with Māori culture, in which collective approaches are valued within daily life. Weiten (2004) stated the following:

> **collectivism involves putting group goals ahead of personal goals and defining one's identity in terms of the group one belongs to** (such as one's family, tribe, work group, social class, caste, and so on)… collectivist cultures place high priority on shared values and resources, cooperation, mutual interdependence, and concern for how one's actions will affect other group members…
>
> Many contemporary societies are in transition, but generally speaking, North American and Western European cultures tend to be individualistic, whereas Asian, African and Latin American cultures tend to be higher in collectivism. (p.65; original emphasis)

The Māori social concept which underpinned the choreography was beneficial in terms of fostering respect for each group member and the demonstration of unconditional positive regard. In Māori cultural terms, positive social approaches were recognised as being fundamental to a therapeutic environment which fostered and enhanced wellbeing. The Māori approaches served to strengthen the outcomes acquired through the archetypal character roles which aligned with individualised therapeutic goals.

Case study: Around the World Through the Seasons
Archetypal significance of the seasons

In Greek mythology, when the goddess of the harvest, Demeter, neglected her worldly domain through despair, it resulted in winter. Her daughter, Persephone, had been abducted and taken to the underworld. While her attention was diverted through searching for her child, her warmth was withdrawn from the earth, and winter arrived for the first time. Her daughter's return and release from enslavement brought about spring. This was the beginning of a cycle, because each year Persephone was obliged to return to the underworld for a period. Winter would come in her absence and spring would arrive upon her return.

Mythologies have suggested that the seasons hold deep psychological significance on an archetypal level, and that the seasons can affect our moods. Also, different psychological tasks have been assigned to each season. Summer is perhaps a time for social connection and celebration, autumn for expressing thankfulness for harvest abundance and making preparation for the coming winter, a period of withdrawal, introspection and soul focus. The joy of Persephone's spring return invites new creative visions that need to be tended through summer to arrive at fruition in the autumn, before the closure of winter.

Historically, there were rituals at solstice and equinox which provided psychological alignment with each of the seasons for whole communities. Summer solstice is the day of the year with the most sunlight, winter solstice being the day with the least, the dates of which are usually around 21 June and 21 December. While the northern hemisphere celebrates summer solstice in June and winter in December, the southern celebrates the opposite. Equinox involves the alignment between the equator and the sun's centre at around 20 March and 22 September. Rituals which have denoted the start of spring and autumn in conjunction with solstice and equinox include Christmas, Easter, Passover, Chinese Moon Festival and Hindu Navaratri.

Developing the seasonal focus in the group process

In approaching the archetypal dimension of the seasons in dance arts, the journey began with a brainstorm to discover the different kinds of associations that each season held for the group members. There was a drawing out of factual and intuitive knowledge followed by Internet searches for related images. The participants then each created a collage in response to their preferred season which brought them to life visually to be celebrated. It was interesting to discover that there was an even spread in preferences across the four seasons by group members, with reasons being offered for the choices made; these included temperatures and colours of seasons, associated natural events and social activities, and symbolic references.

Further Internet research took place to discover songs that had a seasonal reference. Participants arrived at a song through which to lead a dance in the choreography. The choreographic aspects of the dances developed were inspired partly by what we had successfully tried previously with further artistic response to what the different songs suggested. Furthermore, there were connections made with the dance moves in the videos of some of the song recordings, from which we borrowed and adapted to fit our situation. There was an underlying notion of the cycling of the seasons that remained a strong consideration throughout.

As the year progressed, InterACT festival organisers provided a theme of "Around the World," which fitted well with the notion of the seasons being archetypal and global. The dancers then considered which countries resonated as a place to visit in their preferred season and in relationship to their chosen song. We created a world map to show the flight path that would be taken through the course of the choreography. Images were sourced, and we created a slide show that referenced the season and locality of each dance, and which became a digital backdrop. This offered strong visual references to different environments within each season, which also strengthened the connection with the archetypal process. Table 6.3 presents a summary of the course that the dance performance took for the eight participants through the seasons, songs and localities.

Table 6.3 Participants' choices of seasons, songs and localities

Participant	Season	Song	Locality
LY	Winter	"Frozen" (Anderson-Lopez, K. and Lopez, R., vocals Menzel, I., 2013)	Paris, France
JM	Winter	"White Wedding" (Idol, B. and Stevens, S., vocals Idol, B., 1982)	New York, United States
SH	Spring	"Avalanche" Thomas, D. and Houston, J., vocals Hillsong United, 2011)	Southern Alps, New Zealand
MA	Spring	"Raindrops Keep Falling on My Head" (Bacharach, B. and David, H., vocals Thomas, B., 1969)	London, England
PA	Summer	"Hot, Hot, Hot" (Cassell, A., vocals Venga Boys, 2013)	Surfer's Paradise, Australia
LI	Summer	"Under the Boardwalk" (Resnick, A. and Young, K., vocals Midler, B., 1988)	California, United States
EN	Autumn	"Earth Song" (Jackson M., 1995)	Fiji, Pacific Islands
JO	Autumn	"Royals" (O'Connor, J. and Little, J., vocals Lorde, 2013)	Auckland, New Zealand

There was a strong focus on individual pathways within the performance developments and choreography, with each person participating through a series of choices and artistic contributions. At the same time, the group process was highly collaborative, creative and cohesive arriving at choreography that, like the seasons, was cyclic and flowing. The artistic and group processes, as well as the onstage presentation, reflected a sense of unity of the whole of the seasons.

Dance 1 began under blue stage lights to denote winter in Paris where the dancers were statue-like, dormant and iced-over. The lead dancer (LY) became one of the troupe and the catalysing role was taken by a person who was able to move on foot to touch each of the dancers in turn. As each was touched, they sprang to life and moved toward the middle of the floor to meet their dance partner (Figure 6.1). We had advanced to a place where there was a shared ownership of the performance as a whole; however, the acknowledged creative director of the dance was LY.

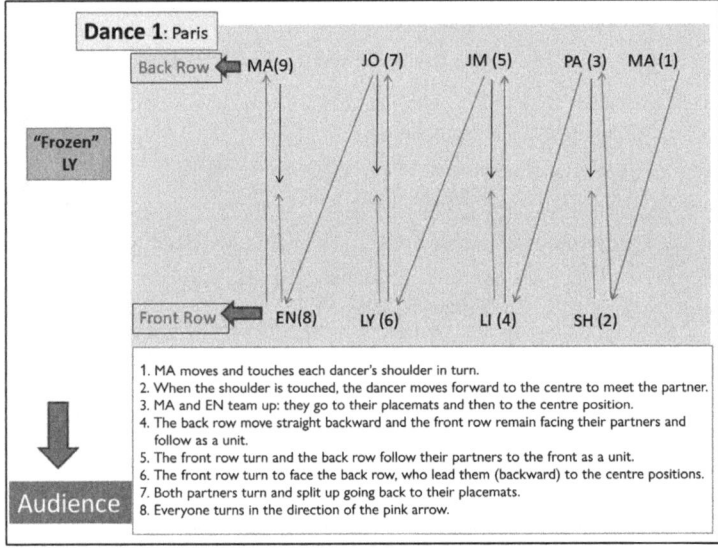

Figure 6.1 Dance 1 floor plan

We journeyed on to New York and a white winter wedding. Similarly, in dance 2 the official author and leader of the dance (JM) had become a member of the troupe and another pair led the way through the symbolic archway (Figure 6.2). The physical positioning and movement of the dancers through the course of the entire choreography was carefully considered so that each person had moments to shine and be acknowledged JM had opportunities to perform his favourite moves of wheelchair spins in dance 3 with the progression into spring.

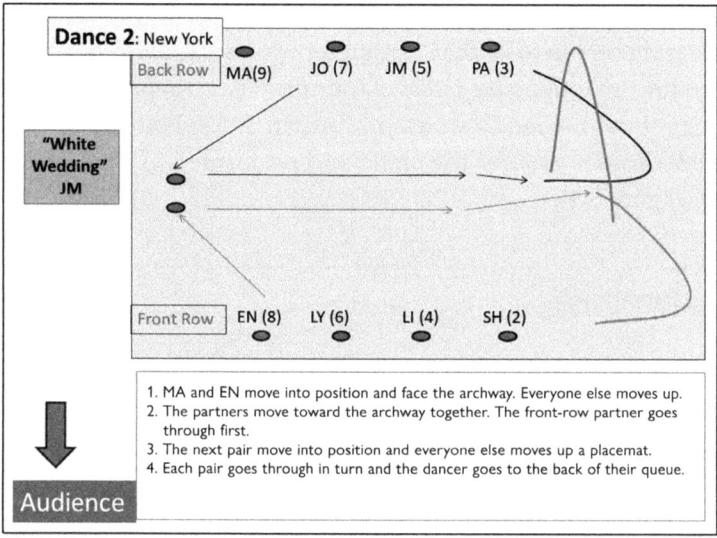

Figure 6.2 Dance 2 floor plan

Progression into spring was conceptualised by SH for whom the ideal location for a metaphorical avalanche, as in her song, was the Southern Alps of *Aotearoa* (New Zealand). SH brought us all back across the globe for dance 3, in which there was something of a circular tango between dance pairs under green stage lighting (Figure 6.3).

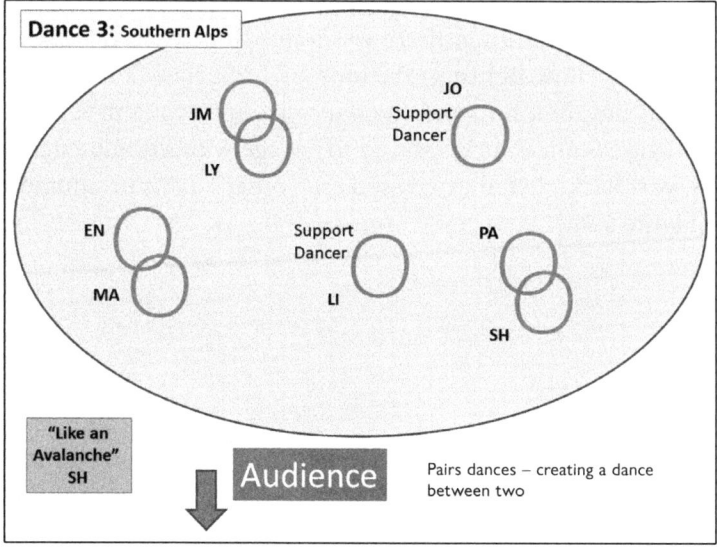

Figure 6.3 Dance 3 floor plan

There was another aspect of spring to be explored: that of rain, and MA found London to be the location for whimsical showers. The tango shifted into an interactive circle of four people, perhaps reminiscent of folk dances of England's streets in former times. Four other dancers formed a square around the circle and performed in time with each other (Figure 6.4).

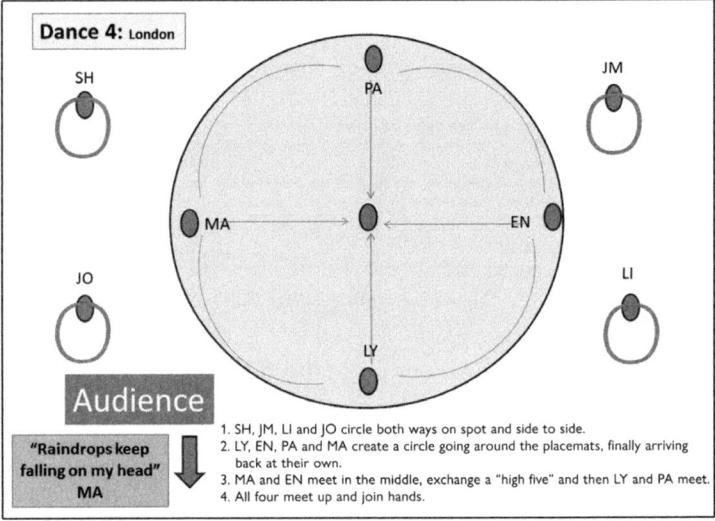

Figure 6.4 Dance 4 floor plan

In moving on to summer, there was a lineup across the back of the stage under yellow lighting. PA took us to Surfer's Paradise beach which was hot, hot, hot, and the dance troupe brought heat toward the audience. Some dancers stayed to engage with the audience while others went back, then they crossed each other's paths in summertime play (Figure 6.5).

EXPRESSIVE DANCE MOVEMENT   111

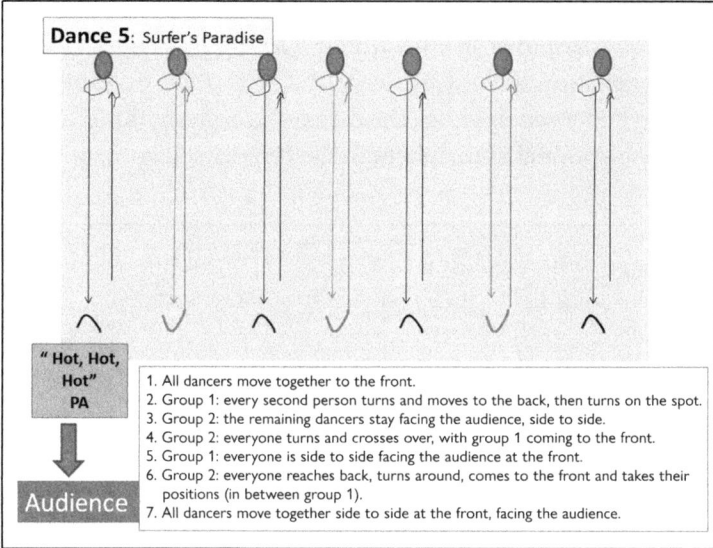

Figure 6.5 Dance 5 floor plan

LI took us under the boardwalk on the sunny shores of California where the playtime partying continued. They travelled concurrently with a partner across the stage and each took a turn of weaving under and around the archway poles for a moment under the spotlight (Figure 6.6).

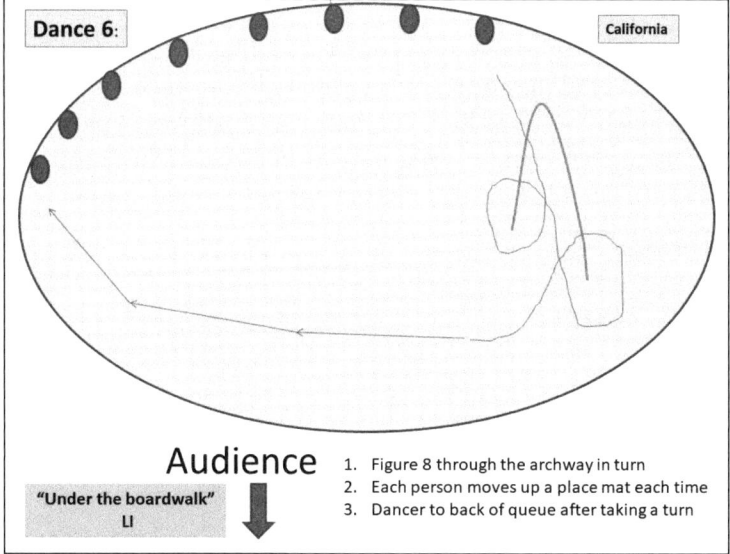

Figure 6.6 Dance 6 floor plan

Autumn brought a journey back to the home shores of *Aotearoa*, but not without a stopover in Fiji, which was the birthplace of EN. We began to transition toward winter with the soulful, tuneful words of Earth Song under red lighting. The dance was both rhythmic and cyclic, bringing the seasonal atmosphere to the forefront (Figure 6.7).

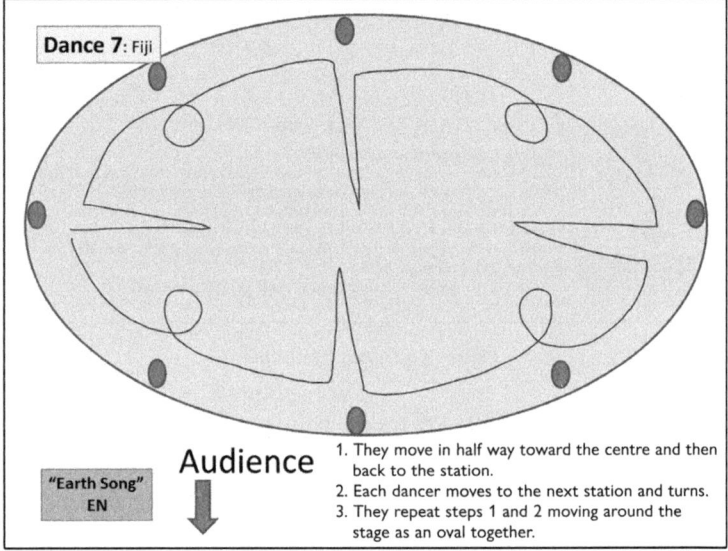

Figure 6.7 Dance 7 floor plan

Back in Auckland through the creative directions of JO, we connected with our roots and the notions of autumn richness and holding queenly power through the song "Royals." There was a pathway of pairs created toward the audience and a zigzag away to be a part of the group lineups (Figure 6.8). Our journey had reached home—completion—and there was triumph in what we had achieved.

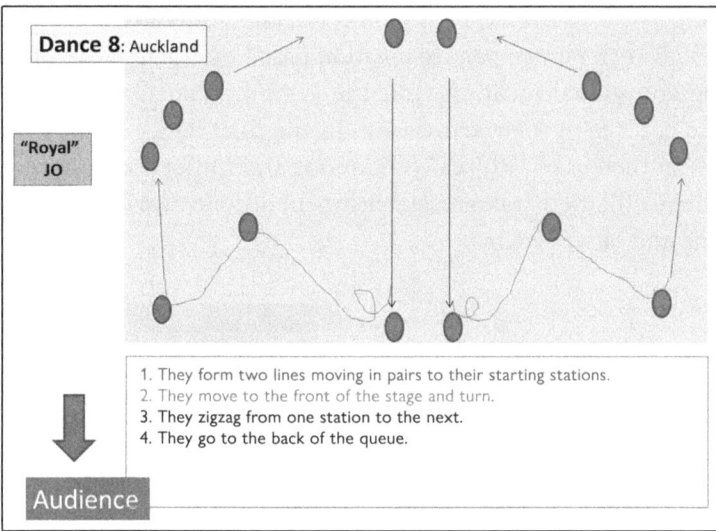

Figure 6.8 Dance 8 floor plan

There had been less emphasis placed on physical acts supporting physiotherapy goals in "Around the World Through the Seasons," but the process had opened up to greater possibilities on other levels. The notion of collectivism (Weiten 2004) was less overt but more integrated in the way that the group took shared ownership of the choreography for the entire performance. The dancers supported each other in lead roles for the best outcome of the intended dance expression. Each person had opportunities to show their strengths and to shine as a leader within the overall performance. The level of collaboration and mutual respect to achieve a shared desired outcome had become more strongly developed.

The benefits of the process were more holistically balanced, as the connection between mind and body was perhaps more synchronised than in "Legends of Maui." There was greater creativity and complexity in the developmental process of the choreography in order to demonstrate appropriate expressions of songs and attitudes that were reflective of the seasons. Embodiment was now a stronger physical component in terms of holding oneself in a fitting posture and making the appropriate choreographic moves (Figure 6.9). This was cognitively engaging and demanding, and required assistance from the staff-crew to reach the performance hopes of the dancers involved. There was a strong sense of self-expression and the claiming of personal identity through each person's dance creation based on their choice of season, song and global location, and the symbols that they attributed to these choices in their artmaking. In the final dance to the powerful musical themes of "Royals" (O'Connor and Little, vocals Lorde 2013; Figure 6.10), there was a reestablishment of collective identity, of being home and of being Kiwi.

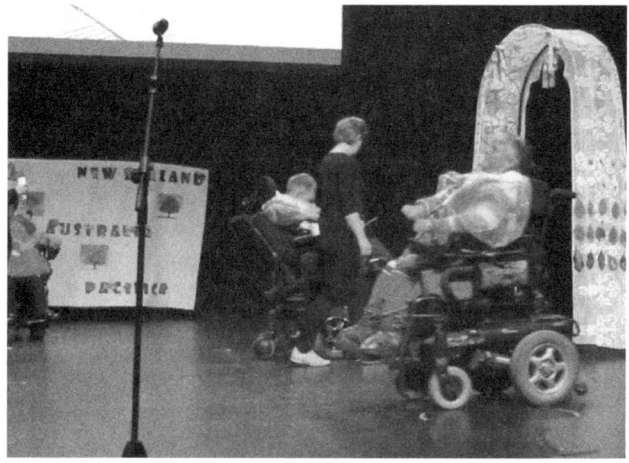

Figure 6.9 Embodying the role in dance 6 (see insert for colour version)

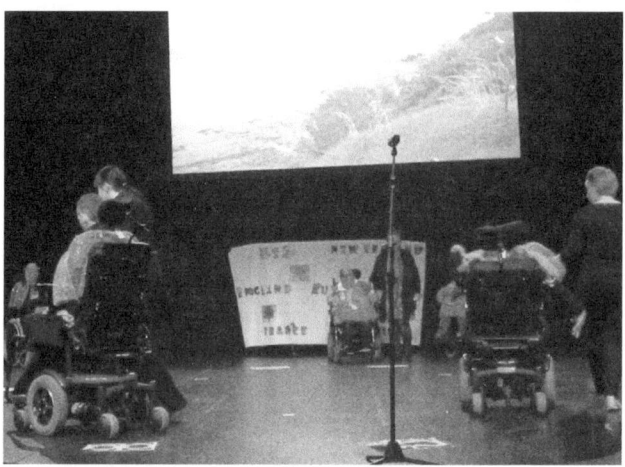

Figure 6.10 Arriving home to Aotearoa (New Zealand) and "queenly power" in the final dance

Conclusion

The two dance performances demonstrated the holistic benefits of working with multimodal arts therapy processes which centre around dance. They demonstrated that dance can support physiotherapy mobility goals within a multidisciplinary setting. Using archetypal approaches as a focus for the developmental processes toward performance created a strong therapeutic basis connected with individual therapy goals. Social connection was enhanced, leading to greater therapeutic benefits.J

CHAPTER 7

Drama

> **Keywords:** archetypal cards, sexuality, individuation, shadow, men's group, video review, performance

In the two case studies presented here, there was a collaborative developmental process which evolved over a number of sessions. Although spontaneous and organic in the way the storylines emerged, the dramas can be recognised as having followed the archetypal pattern that Jung (1964) described in relationship to myths which feature a king, which he suggested denoted the initial stage of individuation. Archetypal cards (Myss 2003) were used as a basis for character development in both dramas, where the second drama built upon the first, and through which a progression can be seen in how the group utilised the symbolic aspects. The group members developed artistic skills and greater therapeutic engagement alongside recognised personal development.

Introduction of dramatherapy within the context

The drama group originated in response to the specific needs of a group of men living in a similar area. Because of transport problems, they had generally been unable to access regular groups. They had made a specific request for a drama group in their home area. They were also interested in music and particularly wanted any groups to meet a need for social interaction.

In response to information gathered, an opportunity was established which was specifically for men and their interests. This was for two hours fortnightly involving less travel than weekly sessions. Drama was the key modality and included development of characters and narrative, costuming, prop making, and sometimes the use of symbols and art materials as a means of response and self-expression. Music was incorporated as a warm-up using percussion instruments, guitar and recorded songs through YouTube. Shared lunch took place as a half-hour component of the session, which provided an opportunity for informal socialising.

This group of men had a range of physical, intellectual and developmental disabilities, and were also of diverse backgrounds and ethnicities. However, they had the ability to take up roles and enact them, and to enter into the complexities of human existence in relationship dynamics created through characterisation. Landy (2009) stated:

> Human beings are role takers and role players by nature. That is the abilities to imagine oneself as another and to act like the other are essentially unlearned and genetically programmed... Human beings strive towards balance and harmony and...have the capacity to accept the consequences of living with ambivalence and paradox. (p.67)

Within the group process and dynamic, it was possible to hold and play out light and shadow, accord and discord, and to develop a dramatic symphony with numerous threads not necessarily in harmony, but with each aspect essential to the wholeness of the group.

The visual dimensions of the drama approaches used within the context were particularly significant to self-expression and role development for the men. Few members of the group were able to participate in full verbal dialogue due to dysarthria or cognitive conditions which were a part of their disabilities. The selection of archetypal cards (Myss 2003), costumes, symbols and props gave individualised authorship through which each participant brought their own dramatic character into being. Even those men who had constricted upper limbs and were non-verbal were able to indicate their choices through eye movements and facial expressions. While the visual aspect of character development took place independently, the naming of the characters, story development and writing of the narrative took place collaboratively. Different scenarios were tried and tested until there was full agreement by the group.

Support staff played a key role in the collaborative process as they held knowledge relevant to the personal histories and cultures of different group members. They also contributed knowledge from their own cultures with which group members could identify.

Their contribution helped provide a culturally enriched environment. The celebration of cultures extended into the social lunch period, where everyone brought along favourite foods to share with each other and there was enjoyment in the opportunity to try new things. Cultural diversity emerged as an underlying theme in "The King-Knight's Daughter" and "The International Convention of the Pacific."

Case study: Drama of *The King-Knight's Daughter*

Archetypal Cards (Myss 2003) proved to be a very useful resource in both dance and drama groups as they captured the imagination in a way that stimulated unexpected and significant dynamics. The drama of *The King-Knight's Daughter* is an example of how archetypes can write their own stories in a phenomenological way. "Archetypes…[are] 'Gods' that have the power to guide human destiny" (Mitchell 1994, p.15). There was a sense that the archetypes lay dormant within the psyche of each of the participants, awaiting their awakening through connection with the cards.

In working with the client group of people who had physical disabilities, one card was generally discovered to be insufficient to personal requirements for characterisation. There was a deep hunger to connect with, and engage in, archetypal roles. Having arrived at a table which offered a vibrant feast, narrowing the decision down to one choice seemed impossible. However, by combining two cards, the participants were able to personalise an archetypal character that was multidimensional and which could satisfy a hearty appetite. From this, it was possible to make a significant collective therapeutic journey which brought the characters to a larger-than-life status and took in multiple themes.

The drama developments of *The King-Knight's Daughter* took place over a period of ten fortnightly sessions and produced a video recording which could be reviewed and celebrated. This video provided an initial exploration into potential processes in dramatic enactment and became the platform for a further drama which included a public performance.

The group was made up of nine men who had disabilities through cerebral palsy, stroke, blindness, congenital conditions and developmental disorders. Two of the men were able to speak clearly. One of these men had expressed interest in becoming a playwright. He was able to have significant input to the script. Three men could articulate in words and brief phrases and the remaining four were predominantly non-verbal. All but two of the men were confined to a wheelchair. A group of staff provided support in developing the narrative, helped with mobility to use different areas of the room, carried out deeds from the script, assisted in putting on costumes and became the voice of the character where required. The arts space used was a large converted warehouse with carpeted floors and fold-away furniture, which made it possible to create sets in different parts of the room and journey between them.

To begin the creative process, each participant chose two archetypal cards which had been laid out on a table for viewing. In some instance the images resonated and in others the archetypal titles were the key, and sometimes both were important. The narrative for both the light and shadow attributes from the cards were read aloud so that participants gained further understanding of the archetypal qualities, both positive and negative, and decided how they might work with their two cards. With the help of the group, participants arrived at a name for their character and then took time to select costumes and individual props that would aid their enactment.

The range of characters which emerged brought both amusement and excitement as the group members contemplated what journey they might make together and the storytelling that could emerge. Two of the men had chosen to take the roles of women. One man put forward the characteristic of devilment and the other of wise goodness. Another participant combined the archetypes of "victim" and "storyteller"; however, then he added the word "killer." Not surprisingly, there was a king; however, he also held the role of a heroic questing knight. There was a messiah-prince, offering a potential reason for a quest in the form of a pilgrimage. Within the diversity of characters, there was the suggestion of people from different kingdoms or lands, which fed into the story development and full naming of the cast, which was as follows:

- King-Knight **Bob** from the land of **The Horse People** with his horse **Bill**
- Warrior-Pioneer **Tupu**
- Detective-Avenger **Tim Simms** from **Scotland Yard**
- Rescuer-Companion **Captain V.**

- Artist-Trickster **Jackson**
- Prostitute-Guide **Roxanne**
- Victim-Storyteller-Killer **Cruise**
- Messiah-Prince **David** from the land of **The Rivers**
- Scribe-Angel **Maria**

Through a piece-by-piece process of experimentation with costuming, roles and scenario options, the story unfolded and consolidated into a script. The following is an abbreviation of the original, which involved a narrator and character voices that were provided by the actors themselves or their staff assistants. The actors moved to the different sets following the narrator's cues and embodied the roles of their characters while taking part in the actions of the story in the following manner:

- Set 1: Kingdom of The Horse People

  The King Knight Bob sets out from his kingdom in the land of The Horse People. He rides his horse, Bill, to meet with the wise Messiah-Prince David who lives in the far-away land of The Rivers.

- Set 2: Mount Tongariro

  As he reaches the Mountains of Tongariro it is almost nightfall, and the sky is very dark and stormy. The wind blows dirt into his face and eyes. Thunder scares his horse, Bill, who bolts and does not stop running until he comes to a cliff and a long slope down into darkness. King-Knight Bob climbs down and leads Bill along the edge of the cliff until they come to a cave where they both can shelter until morning.

- Set 3: The Cave

  The King falls asleep, and when he wakes up, his horse Bill is standing nearby with the Warrior-Pioneer Tupu sitting on his back. Tupu says, "This is my cave. Who are you? What are you doing here?"

  King-Knight Bob informs Warrior-Pioneer Tupu of his intended quest and explains how he came to be in the cave. He asks for the return of his horse. Initially Tupu is hesitant to return the horse; however, King-Knight Bob pays him generously, in gold, for the overnight use of his cave. Tupu then suggests that the king employ the services of Prostitute-Guide Roxanne to show him the way through the mountains. Trustingly King-Knight Bob pays Roxanne in advance and then is led down an uncertain path. Eventually she instructs King-Knight Bob to follow the river and she rides away. As she does, he thinks he can hear her laughing to herself.

- Set 4: The Waterfall

It is not long before King-Knight Bob reaches the end of the river as it goes over a steep bank in the form of a waterfall with no way to follow it any further. Fortunately for him, his wife Queen Charlotte has been worried about her husband making the journey alone and has sent out two of his loyal subjects, the Avenger-Detective Tim Simms and the Rescuer-Companion Captain V., to check. They have been following his tracks and catch up with him. Captain V. announces their mission to the king, and Tim Simms suggests that he will arrest Roxanne for the trouble she has caused. However, the king declines this suggestion as he would rather they focus their efforts on finding Messiah-Prince David. Tim Simms uses his astute detective skills to help them find the way and soon they arrive at The Land of the Rivers.

- Set 5: The Land of the Rivers (The Inn)

When they reach the land of The Rivers of the Messiah-Prince, they stop at an Inn for food and refreshments, and they find the Prostitute-Guide Roxanne already at the Inn. The Detective-Avenger Tim Simms is quick to place her under arrest. But King-Knight Bob says, "You can go free as long as you give back the money you took from me." Some of it has already been spent, but she returns the remainder.

As they sit in the inn eating their meal, the Artist-Trickster Jackson comes and plays them a song. His song hypnotises them and they put their heads down on the table and fall asleep. He is just about to take the king's wallet but is interrupted by the Victim-Storyteller-Killer Cruise, who has been watching from the corner of the room. "Off you go, villain! Leave that wallet alone! I know what you're up to!" he shouts.

The king and his companions wake up as the Artist-Trickster Jackson runs away into the street, leaving the storyteller Cruise to tell the tale. The king takes money from his wallet and hands Cruise a bundle of notes thanking him for his kindness and honesty. He tells him that he will provide a further payment for the successful finding of the Messiah-Prince David. Cruise suggests that the messiah-prince will be in his hiding place and sets out to discover the location. Prostitute-Guide Roxanne indicates that she knows where he is and again requests payment in advance. Cruise reluctantly hands over most of the money that the king had given him, remembering her very recent betrayal. This time, however, she is true to her word.

- Set 6: The River Boat

The Victim-Storyteller-Killer Cruise carefully climbs onto the riverboat which is the hiding place of Messiah-Prince David, making sure that no one sees him. Messiah-Prince David welcomes him and is pleased to hear the news that the king has come to seek his advice. A meeting is arranged for the morning when Cruise will take the king and his companions to a secret location in the forest.

- Set 7: Secret Location in the Forest

Messiah-Prince David is with Scribe-Angel Maria whom he sometimes consults when uncertain, particularly about women's matters. The king describes his problem of his daughter, Princess Aroha, having three suitors: the father of one with whom he had matched her owned the finest horses in the world; one with whom she had fallen in love, whose inheritance would be spices; and a third from the land of precious gems. The king looks very worried and clearly quite perplexed.

Messiah-Prince David thinks for a moment while the king sits sighing. Soon the wise messiah-prince has an answer for the king and smiles. He suggests that the king ask each prince to demonstrate his best strengths and let Princess Aroha choose who she should marry for herself. This is most likely to make her happy and will therefore be a good match for the kingdom. The messiah-prince asks Scribe-Angel Maria for her thoughts on the matter who affirms that this will also be agreeable to Queen Charlotte. The king is relieved to have an answer and thanks the messiah-prince.

The king feels very happy as he and his party make the long journey home to The Land of the Horse People, knowing that the solution he has been given will be well received by both his daughter and his wife, and that it will be best for his kingdom.

Therapeutic significance of the story

There were a number of themes of empowerment that the men were able to explore collectively through their chosen characters and the roles that unfolded within the story. Some men related to being a significant figure within a community, including those of esteemed regal power, wisdom and authority, benevolence, guardianship and wealth; others related to more everyday dimensions of honesty, villainy, sexuality, seduction, marriage, parenthood, masculinity and femininity, sacredness, freedom of choice and decision making. These were aspects of our shared human experience that were less available in daily life for the group members because of their disabilities. The drama provided an opportunity to experience what it might be like to hold various positions of responsible and irresponsible power and explore the social dynamics that resulted from different role interactions.

The different sets—kingdoms, rivers, caves, waterfalls and a secret location in the forest—bore archetypal reference to fairy tales. Jung (1964) suggested that the king and the events that take place toward him in fairy tales often "describe…[the] initial stage in a process of individuation" (p.167). In classical fairy tales, this takes place more symbolically: "a monster steals all the women, children, horses and wealth of the kingdom; or that a demon keeps the king's army or his ship from proceeding on its course" (p.167). Our own story appeared to have followed a similar pattern of adversity in a milder form, where the king had a dilemma for which he needed to seek advice, and his progress was thwarted by the Prostitute-Guide Roxanne who left him facing the unknown. Traditionally, "one finds that magic or a talisman that can cure the misfortune of the king or his country" (p.167). This was present in the quest to find the Messiah-Prince David and the wisdom that he was able to provide.

The group found the drama process and video outcomes very satisfying and they were eager to use these approaches to develop a new story. The notions of individuation were extended through the next drama of *The International Convention of the Pacific*, where the men seemed to have progressed into greater symbolic depths. In this, there was an expanded interest in the shadow side of the archetypes, along with more confidence and humour. They were also able to achieve their goals of performing on a public stage.

Case study: Drama of *The International Convention of the Pacific*

The group of men who had been involved in the drama of *The King-Knight's Daughter* established a new drama that extended the range of roles and experiences. One member left the group and another arrived, maintaining the group at nine. Once again, the men used archetypal cards to create their characters using both the visual images and the words to assist in their choices. There was a greater sense of confidence, adventure and humour in the new characters that arrived. The men had seen the potential through the development of the previous drama and clearly wanted to go further with their explorations of roles, social dynamics and storytelling, and to have fun with it. It became obvious that there was a growing interest in exploring the shadow side along with the more noble aspects of humanity. Myss (2003) has suggested that:

> All archetypes have shadow manifestations as well as positive aspects… (p.5)
>
> They take an active role as guardians and inner allies, awakening you when you're in danger of falling into destructive behaviour… (p.4)
>
> When you learn to recognize…[a destructive] pattern instead of ignoring or denying its presence, it becomes your friend and helper. (p.5)

Most of the participants wanted to test out a different role from their previous one. Some people moved toward an opposite role, while others built on a personal theme. They were keen to experiment and to extend their role repertoire, or to find and claim the different archetypal aspects within their psyche. Archetypal characters chosen in the two dramas are compared and contrasted in Table 7.1.

Table 7.1 Comparison between roles in the two dramas

Role in previous drama	New card choices
Scribe-Angel Maria	Thief-Hero
King-Knight Bob	Hedonist-Lover
Prostitute-Guide Roxanne	Visionary-Priest
Artist-Trickster Jackson	Knight-Shapeshifter
Rescuer-Companion Captain V.	Engineer-Vampire
Messiah-Prince David	Father-King
Detective-Avenger Tim Simms	Liberator-Judge
Warrior-Pioneer Tupu	Samaritan-Rescuer
(New group member; no previous role)	Nature Lover (one card only)

In recognition of the multicultural nature of the group, the idea was posed that a country of origin could be attributed to each of the new characters, which might then assist with the process of naming them and in the development of the story. It was an opportunity to express one's own cultural background or to explore another culture. The group was made up of the following cultures: Māori, New Zealand European, Tongan, Samoan, Niuean and Chinese ethnicities. Most group members chose to explore a similar, but different, cultural background to their own. Figures 7.1 to 7.9 show *The International Convention of the Pacific* developmental process in which the steps were as follows:

1. Archetypal cards were chosen.

2. Countries of origin were chosen.

3. Cultures, clothing and names were researched.

4. Names of characters were chosen.

5. Flags of countries were located.

6. Costumes began with colour or a cultural theme.

7. The story was developed.

126 ARTS THERAPIES WITH PEOPLE WITH PHYSICAL DISABILITIES

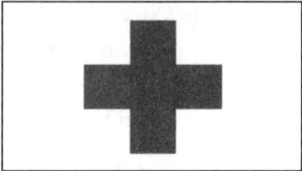

Figure 7.1 **King Tupou**, *the Father-King from Samoa and Tonga; wants the best for his people and all people; costuming: Tongan cloth*

Figure 7.2 **John Cruise**, *the Thief-Hero from California; Hollywood star—has stolen money to give to the poor of Africa; costuming: red, black, brown*

Figure 7.3 **Sultan**, *the Hedonist-Lover from Arabia; travels with "a couple of birds"; holds "parties"; costuming: blue*

Figure 7.4 **Count Ironstein**, *Engineer-Vampire from Madagascar; keeps people captive in a factory; costuming: orange*

Figure 7.5 **Judge Bolyn**, *the Liberator-Judge from Sydney, Australia; uses a plane to rescue people; costuming: red*

DRAMA 127

Figure 7.6 **Night Warrior Zorro**, *the Knight-Shapeshifter from Auckland, New Zealand; travels undetected at night wearing a mask; costuming: blue*

Figure 7.7 **Santino**, *the Samaritan-Rescuer from Argentina; a cowboy who uses a lasso and gun; costuming: red, black, white*

Figure 7.8 **Akiiki**, *the Visionary-Priest from Uganda; performs the "opening blessing" for the conference; costuming: black tunic*

Figure 7.9 **Chef Wong**, *the Nature Lover from China; traveling chef who cooks amazing food; costuming: white shirt and chef's hat*

Bly (2002) stated:

> Archetypal themes are universal, for they can be found in every culture throughout history. But each society reflects them in different ways. The American lover, for example, is far more romantic, erotic and idealised than images portrayed in Asia. By contrast, the shadow, which is aptly acknowledged in European psyche, is relatively ignored by Americans. Unlike other cultures, we do not like to peer directly into the darkness within. Instead we project our shadows onto fiction, movies, or the criminal elements in the world. (p.5)

There were the influences from American films in the story which emerged through the archetypal interests of the group. Perhaps it was easier to project the shadow roles onto other cultures than to relate them to our own. "The shadow is not a pleasant subject to talk about. Human beings have never wanted to talk much about their dark side. If they had wanted to, it wouldn't now be called the shadow" (Bly 2002, p.8).

The exploration of cultures resulted in depth research through Internet sources and a virtual global journey which extended our collective world view. The men sought to create authentic cultural dress in their costumes. Flags became props which were hand-held or attached to wheelchairs as symbols of their characters' cultural identities. This extended the sense of being connected to wider humanity with a sense of each person having an important role and contribution to make.

Once again, the story had centred around a king who had a holy advisor. This time no female characters had emerged. Our verbally articulate script writer had moved on through external circumstances, and we created a drama that relied entirely on narration and the presentation and movements of the actors to tell the story. In this drama there were only two locations involved: the Island of the Dark Swamp and the Beautiful Island of Frangipani. In the previous drama there had been six sets. The actors were able to focus more on embodiment which was detectable in posture, body language, facial expressions and auric vitality.

The story of two islands and King Tupou's Convention

The following is an abbreviation of the narration which was read aloud while the characters acted their parts:

King Tupou lives in his palace on the beautiful Island of Frangipani between Tonga and Samoa, and he is the Father-King of both countries. He has called a convention of leaders from around the world because he wants to create a better life for Pacific peoples. Waiting with him for the arrival of the guests is Priest Akiiki, visionary-priest from Uganda, and Chef Wong, the nature lover from China, who is preparing the food.

They have advised everybody who is coming to use the longer route to avoid going near the Island of the Dark Swamp. Lately there had been strange happenings and people going missing there. The island is known for its all-night parties, and King Tupou and Priest Akiiki had concerns that some of the travellers might ignore the warning.

The first traveller to cross the waters toward Frangipani Island is Judge Bolyn, the liberator-judge from Sydney, a pilot who flies over the Island of the Dark Swamp and lands safely. Next is Santino, the samaritan-rescuer from Argentina who travels by boat and takes his horse with him. He heeds the warning of the king going by the long route and makes it safely to the convention. Māori Zorro, the knight-shape-shifter from Auckland, New Zealand, also travels by boat taking his horse with him. They arrive safely.

The king is very happy to see them and welcomes them, but he is soon worried again when other travellers are overdue. Travelling all the way from Arabia is Sultan, the hedonist-lover, with some of his harem. He likes to party and has heard about the Island of the Dark Swamp. He decides to ignore the king's warning. The Sultan travels by boat with another party-goer who he has met on the way, John Cruise, the thief-hero from California. He had been told stories about a possible *taniwha* or Loch Ness monster. He just laughed. However, when they go by the shorter route and stop at the Island of the Dark Swamp to see if there are any parties, they soon find out that the king is right!

Unbeknown to everyone, the island has a cave in the side of a hill which reaches down to below the level of the sea. The cave has been taken over by Count Ironstein, the engineer-vampire from Madagascar. He takes them captive for his dark experiments in his laboratory where he farms human blood.

With the two travellers now several hours overdue, the king shares his fears with Judge Bolyn, Samaritan-Cowboy Santino and Māori Zorro, and the three set out on a rescue mission by plane.

Night-Warrior Māori Zorro uses his special shape-shifter powers to get inside the underground cave and to quietly free the two rogues from their chained captivity. Then he opens the door for the other rescuers. Samaritan-Cowboy Santino uses his gun and lasso to apprehend Count Ironstein, and Judge Boyd arrests him with handcuffs. They chain him up in the place where he had been holding his captives. The police are phoned and soon arrive to take him away.

Then all five men climb into Judge Bolyn's plane and arrive safely at the Island of the King and the convention. Here, Thief-Hero John Cruise passes over money and the Sultan from Arabia passes over jewels as a way of apologising to the king. Father-King Tupou is happy because this will help his peoples of the Pacific, and the convention turns out to be a very big success.

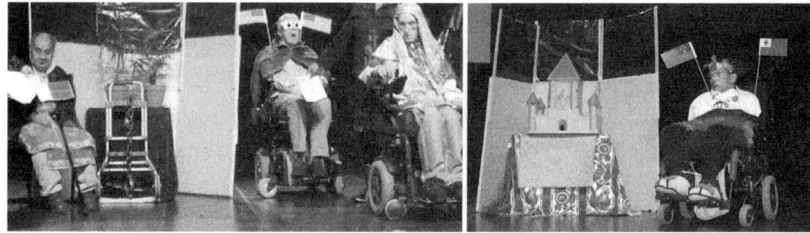

Figure 7.10 The actors in their public performance at InterACT Festival in Auckland (see insert for colour version)

Therapeutic development in the second drama

Once again, there is a king involved in the story and his kingdom is affected by sinister shadow dimensions which, this time, were on a par with those described by Jung (1964) in "a monster" (p.167) who stole some of the king's guests for evil purposes, and which immobilises planned events. There were three rogues created in which individual character development was focused primarily on the shadow. There was a sense of reckless abandonment in the way in which the three rogues were presented, none of whom showed any regard for the concerns expressed by the king.

Jung (1964) stated:

The shadow…shows up…as an impulsive or inadvertent act. Before one has time to think, the evil remark pops out, the plot is hatched, the wrong decision is made, and one is confronted with results that were never intended or consciously wanted. (p.169)

The engineer-vampire was conducting diabolical experiments with no care for humanity or any kind of consequences; the hedonist-lover had collected women for his pleasure and dripped with the ostentatious wealth of his sultan status; and the thief-hero who had justified robbing the rich, was also a winning poker player. It seemed that time would tell whether the sultan would also fall prey to the thief's antics.

The cure by magic or talisman that Jung suggested (p.167), in this case, took place through Māori Zorro, the knight-shape-shifter from Auckland, New Zealand, who demonstrated special powers and freed the captives. The two liberated rogues then experienced shame for their negative shadow acts and made an adjustment by showing a positive side of the shadow (p.168) or their more socially favourable side. The lifestyles of both characters suggested that their shadow sides were dominant, and the king was willing to overlook the origins of the gifts that they presented, in order to enhance the lives of his beloved people. This was a shadowing of his light attributes.

There was an interesting balance created within the cast: three host-providers dominated by light attributes; three villains who were dominated by shadow qualities; and three rescuers who perhaps resided in the space in between, with their trickery, guns and physical approaches. The story arrived at an unspoken understanding that people present with shades of grey rather than black and white, with the light attributes coloured by the shadow.

Conclusion

Benefits were evident on multiple levels including the advancement in maturity within the artistic therapeutic process, which Jung suggested related to the archetypal role of the king and individuation. The increased playfulness of the dramatists in the second drama showed a high level of confidence and command of the processes, and that disabilities were no barrier to learning techniques and creating dramatic significance. The sense of achievement in performing on stage at InterACT Festival was immeasurable, as this was a validation of significance and worthiness that the group had rarely experienced in the course of their day-to-day lives. The group went on to explore other ways of approaching drama and music, as presented in the next chapter.

CHAPTER 8

Music

Keywords: mythology, *Te Whare Tapa Whā*, recorded music, percussion instruments, transformation, metaphor, memories

In offering therapeutic opportunities for people who had disabilities, music crept into the arena quietly at first, grew organically and became a key component of multimodality, through which significant benefits of engagement with music could be identified. It would be difficult to imagine the successes of multimodal arts therapy without the driving forces of music and the intrinsic soul connections that it held for the client group.

The development of music as a therapeutic dimension of service is reviewed here, and two cases studies are provided which explored the capacity of music to come unexpectedly to the forefront in ways that were transformational. The two case studies offer quite different views of how music can lead the way in a therapeutic process.

Music has been recognised as archetypal within itself, and in "Voices of the Māori Gods," percussion instruments brought mythology to life in a new way within a drama process. "Yellow Bird" explores the way in which the song arose in a group process, providing metaphors and significance.

The arrival of music as a primary modality

Music was the second modality to be introduced within the rehabilitation context, which began with individual art therapy. Music was occasionally utilised within sessions where a person showed interest. The focus on music as a primary modality had simple beginnings when service users and staff were offered an opportunity to participate in a

Christmas choir. Within a few weeks the choir had performed at events, and there was interest in developing it in the longer term as a form of music therapy. A weekly choir group was offered. Each person who joined chose a song meeting the criteria that it should be uplifting and hold universal appeal. This began the development of a group repertoire of songs. Inspirational Choir was established as a weekly group where songs were played on a guitar and accompanied by a sing-along with recorded artists through YouTube.

Percussion instruments were introduced to broaden the musical and therapeutic possibilities. These instruments provided a means of self-reflection and introduction at the beginning of session, of tuning in with each other's sounds and rhythms, and served as a form of musical engagement during the singing. Other instruments made available included a guitar, ukulele and keyboard, which were selected as a regular mode of musical improvisation for some group members.

Research into choirs as a form of music therapy appeared limited at the time; however, the benefits were obvious through the way in which participants engaged with certain songs that held resonance and memories for them. There were delighted facial expressions, tears and outbursts of spontaneous singing from people who had previously been mostly non-verbal. Quite separately, the University of Auckland had begun a similar choir called CeleBRation with research being conducted into the benefits of participation for people who had Parkinson's disease or were in recovery from stroke (Buetow *et al.* 2014). There were similarities in approaches to those of our own choir, which was for people who had cerebral palsy, other forms of brain injury and diverse disabilities. This alignment strengthened our position and confidence in offering choir as a form of therapy.

In describing the benefits of a singing group for people who had Parkinson's disease, Buetow *et al.* (2014) suggested:

> [Quality of life] QoL depends on interactions between variables that include musical qualities of the songs—such as their rhythm, harmony, melody and lyrics—to which people may connect. In turn, context-sensitive social processes may connect…[participants] to others in the singing group in ways that ripple outwards to a musical community and bring that community back in. (p.431)

In using the Arts Therapy 5-Pt Star assessment and self-evaluation to record progress (see Chapter 2), there were indications of similar outcomes for people who had physical disabilities in the broader spectrum. The performances that had been an aspect of our initial Christmas choir remained a strong goal of the choir group, in which our stated focus was on creating community. Audiences were invited to both witness and participate, with the performers taking the roles of singing leaders. At public events, there were significant shifts in roles from being marginalised, discounted and unappreciated, to becoming recognised and celebrated as providers of culturally enriching experiences. There was validation as being valuable contributors to the wider community.

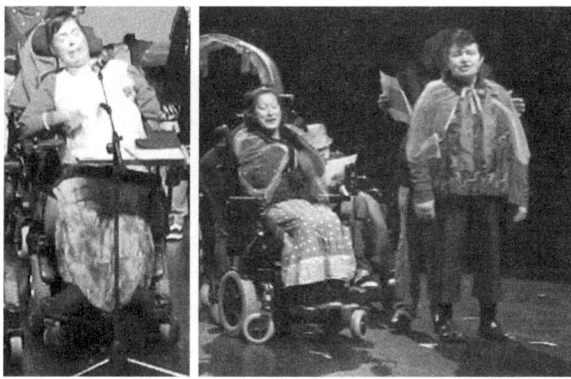

Figure 8.1 Singing on stage at InterACT Festival

A second group, Percussion and Voice, was formed. This offered an opportunity, at a more suitable time of day, for people who had very high needs (VHN) status and who found the afternoon timing of the established choir difficult. This group mostly required the assistance of support staff to hold and use instruments; however, even the small tinkling sound of a bell or soft thud of a hand on a bongo could bring an immense sense of achievement and musical enjoyment. Similarly, being able to make tuneful vocal sounds in response to songs for those who found verbal articulation difficult was greatly satisfying. People with profound physical disabilities were able to engage on multiple levels:

- Being immersed in the vibrations of the sounds, connecting emotionally and feeling "a part of it"

- Making vocal sounds which expressed emotional connection and soul

- Creating rhythms using an instrument of choice that expressed "emotions in the moment"
- Being able to reveal uniqueness of personality and identity through choices in songs, instruments and sounds made
- Having culture of origin recognised and honoured by the group through songs, and being able to reconnect with "home"

Swallow (2002) pointed out the archetypal nature of music in the following:

> music, song and dance [may have] preceded language as a means of communication... Many animals have musical utterances [for different communication purposes]... Birds have an inbuilt capacity for song but their music is refined by environmental factors and practice... Evolution would suggest that man has...inherited a capacity for processing music...[which] has been of importance throughout history and in all societies. (pp.41–42)

Music therapy has evolved as a highly specialised field within the arts therapies, perhaps because of the depth and broadness of possibilities (Bunt and Hoskyns 2002; Bruscia 1991; Campbell 1992; Lem 1993; Nordoff and Robbins 1971). As suggested by Nordoff and Robbins, "Music is a world. Everyone of us has...[our] own experiences in that world. There are endless depths, infinite varieties and facets of musical experience for the listener, the student, the performer, the composer, and for the therapist" (p.141).

Music in multimodal arts therapy groups

With the advent of the service expanding into multimodal groups, in most groups music became a key modality. In some forums, music was the focus, and in others it was an invisible river running through and driving other modes of creative expression. Music provided bridges between cultures, articulation where there were no words, and created unity within communal gatherings. The range of approaches grew into an expanded list which included the following:

- Drums and percussion circles
- Group singing with live amped guitar

- Group singing to recorded music or guitar while playing an instrument
- Solo renditions using instruments and voice in individual multimodal sessions
- Responding to music in painting, expressive dance and guided visualisation
- Instrumental sounds to build atmosphere and articulate characters in drama
- Song as metaphor

Bunt and Hoskyns (2002) have formulated the "music therapy spectrum," which "focuses on six approaches that can underpin music therapy practice: physiological, developmental, supportive, psychodynamic, humanistic and transpersonal" (p.44). These focuses can be extended toward the full range of arts therapy modalities used, with a humanist focus being primary.

The humanist approach is characterised by whole-self concepts which are holistic and include the person's social circumstances and environment, and phenomenological notions of here and now and self-growth. Humanist approaches are eclectic through being responsive to potentiality and individual needs (Bunt and Hoskyns 2002, p.44).

The humanist focus aligned with the Māori model for health, *Te Whare Tapa Whā*, which was developed by Mason Durie in 1982 and adopted by the New Zealand Ministry of Health. *Te Whare Tapa Whā* was an holistic approach which conceptualised four aspects within the framework of a *wharenui* meeting house. These aspects were *wairua* (spirit), *tinana* (body), *hinengaro* (mind) and *whanau* (family) (Durie 2001; Manaia 2017, pp.38–39).

Whereas public events were the highlights, the weekly/fortnightly groups involved privately held nurturing spaces of creative self-exploration, psychodynamic process, confidence and skill building, and social development. Within the improvisation of group activities there were places where music unexpectedly rushed forward as a driving river within a process. Two examples are presented here as case studies:

- In "Voices of the Māori Gods," music arose within the development of a drama, where Māori mythology was the focus of archetypal exploration and musical instruments became the voices of the gods.

- In "Yellow Bird," music rushed forward as a metaphor to assist in a brainstorming process within a personal development setting. It was a song that came quietly into someone's mind and was brought into group discussion. Then it asked to be brought out of its archival hiding place to live again and be loved once more; and then again and again.

Within these two different events, music arose as a language, with its own power, and provided solutions which were "fittingly magnificent."

Case study: Voices of the Māori gods

Bunt and Hoskyns (2002) have conceptualised the "essential 'I's of music therapy practice… imagination, intuition, improvisation and intellect… In all working situations we feel it is vital to be aware of the enlivening nature of these processes" (p.45). In seeking to provide an appropriate intervention for an intermodal drama and music group, there was a focus on tapping into the four "I"s within the group, to arrive at a point of social unity, and sounds that brought satisfaction and therapeutic benefits.

The group had been established to provide an opportunity for men living within supported housing at different localities to engage in their preferred modes of arts therapy while also offering a chance to socialise together on a regular basis. The two-hour fortnightly sessions had four components: "meet and greet"; singing with recorded music/ guitar and percussion instruments; "shared international lunch"; and drama and/ or prop making.

The multicultural group was made up of seven men, all of whom were either considered to be non-verbal or limited in ability to use verbal language; however, some were able to sing the words of whole songs. Schlaug, Marchina and Norton (2008) have suggested that two different neural pathways within brain function could explain the ability to sing where speech has been impaired, and factors such as pacing and rhythm can also contribute to the ability to sing. The men had demonstrated varying levels in physical ability in playing musical instruments independently. Support staff played a crucial role through helping the participants to physically engage with their chosen instruments, and they also contributed to the singing.

Although recorded music was enjoyed as a warm-up, greater participation, engagement and connection were evident with the live amped-guitar and vocals. Each of the men had shown moments of deep emotional connection when a particular song resonated for him, with his memories and perhaps his own vibrations. "If the body can respond so decisively to music, it must in some sense be music" (Campbell 1992, p.60). Songs came to be an enlivened beginning to the sessions, during which there were sometimes tears of joy, nostalgia and release.

Some of the men also clearly found liberation and elation in being able to create rhythms with percussion. For some, even the ability to make small sounds independently could bring a significant sense of achievement. There were also pleasures and therapeutic benefits in the collective group sounds made through drumming and percussion. Aluede and Aiwuyo (2002) stated, "In traditional African healing settings, music is used to reduce anticipated pains therapeutically, as is evident in circumcision and orthopaedic (bone-setting) ceremonies… [research has shown that] brief drumming sessions can double alpha wave activities dramatically reducing stress" (p.173).

The multicultural group was made up of three New Zealand Europeans, two from Pacific Islands, one Māori and one Asian. Five of the men used wheelchairs for mobility through the disabilities of cerebral palsy or degenerative health conditions: two used manual chairs pushed by support staff, and three used motorised chairs with head or hand controls for independent mobilisation. Two of the men were able to walk: one used a walking stick after partial paralysis through a stroke; and the other was blind and had a developmental disability, for which he required constant supervision. The age range was between 35 and 65 years, and all of the men needed some support to participate.

Table 8.1 outlines the challenges, abilities and interests of the individuals in relation to musical approaches.

Table 8.1 Participants' musical abilities and interests

Participant code	Vocal/musical participation abilities and interests
A	Affected by severe dysarthria; able to sing along to some songs, and to use percussion and other musical instruments independently; particularly enjoyed creating a drum beat using a stick
B	Affected by severe dysarthria; contributed tuneful vocal sounds in favourite songs; enjoyed using percussion instruments with assistance

C	Non-verbal, sometimes made loud vocal expressions of excitement, happiness or anger; could play keyboard notes independently for brief periods when positioned in an accessible way; could hold and move some of the smaller percussion instruments
D	English as a second language; would sing all of the words of favourite songs audibly; not observed using verbal language in conversation; could hold some smaller instruments and make movements with assistance
E	English as a second language; could speak words and phrases, however rarely did so; would sing along to favourite songs; enjoyed holding and playing instruments with assistance
F	Limited ability to use conversational language; extraordinary talent in music; able to lead using the large drum with perfect rhythm and improvise a strum for guitar while the therapist played the notes; able to play known tunes on keyboard and with mouth organ, and could sing a repertoire of songs
G	Understood minimal English and spoke only Chinese; able to use instruments independently and enjoyed being a drummer

In the Māori story of creation, there were seven brothers in a multitude of 70, each of whom was a god of a different dominion and possessed special powers. Māori Legends: New Zealand in History (2004) introduced the story as follows:

> In the beginning there was no sky, no sea, no earth and no Gods. There was only darkness, only *Te Kore*, the Nothingness… From this nothingness, the primal parents of the Māori came, *Papatuanuku*, the Earth mother, and *Ranginui*, the Sky father.
>
> *Papatuanuku* and *Ranginui* came together, embracing in the darkness, and had 70 male children. These offspring became the gods of the Māori. However, the children of *Papatuanuku* and *Ranginui* were locked in their parents embrace, in eternal darkness, and yearned to see some light. They eventually decided that their parents should be separated, and they had a meeting to decide what should be done.
>
> They considered for a long time… Should Rangi and Papa be killed? Or shall they be forced to separate?

The events that then followed centred around the separation of the parents and the coming of the light *te ao marama*, which allowed the demigods to grow and utilise their powers.

The men in the group found the brotherhood of seven demigods a good fit for their number and were keen to explore the concept of special powers. They also welcomed the opportunity to strengthen their New Zealand identity collectively through Māori cultural engagement. There was easy negotiation toward preferred character roles to arrive at a full cast.

In the succeeding sessions, the story was enacted with narration, and once familiar to them, colourful costumes and props were chosen from the drama wardrobe by each of the actors to further bring his character to life. However, the enactment continued to lack the heightened level of the drama that the story suggested, until each of the men selected a musical instrument to collectively create the "voices of the gods."

Table 8.2 shows the participants' roles and instrument choices.

Table 8.2 Participants' roles and instrument choices

Participant code	Character role in the story	Musical instrument for voice of the god
A	*Tūmatauenga* God of war, hunting, fishing and agriculture	Large bongo drum that made the loud thumping sound of battle announcement
B	*Ruaumoko* God of earthquakes, volcanoes and seasons	Large cymbals and his own loud battle cry of destruction
C	*Tānemahuta* God of forests and birds	Clackers that made the chattering sounds of the forest birds
D	*Haumaitiketike* God of wild food plants	Soft sounds of nature through an organic rattle made of seeds within pods
E	*Rongomatane* God of peace and of cultivated plants	Chimes that made the peaceful sounds of a breeze through the trees
F	*Tāwhirimātea* God of the weather and storms	A loud whooshing sound made by metal balls inside a drum casing
G	*Tangaroa* God of the sea	A tambourine drum that made the rhythm of the ocean waves

The instruments advanced the drama into a conversation between the gods through musical sounds which became the story. The men met in a circle in their costumed finery and communicated through their individual and collective demigod percussive voices. There was presence, sensitivity, attentiveness and embodiment of the characters until the dramatic potential of the story was finally reached.

In the finale of the musical drama there was a sense of the gestalt, of integration with the sum being greater than its parts. There was completeness in terms of social unity and a strong sense of pride among the men through having performed an essential role in a significant Māori cultural story. Music had proved to be the ultimate transforming agent in the creative therapeutic process.

Case study: Yellow Bird

Plato in Cameron (1997) stated, "Music has the capacity to touch the innermost reaches of the soul and give flight to the imagination" (p.161). Furthermore, we carry music from the soulful times of our lives within the recesses of our memories. For one person, a song can carry a myriad of meanings and connections to places, people, eras and events; and for a group, the multiplicity of these factors. A song can spring to life again in any place and at any time. It can serve as a metaphor that has layers of meaning that originate in the archetypal depths of the unconscious mind.

A group of four people had been sitting around a table in wheelchairs at the end stages of a research project, which they were preparing as a PowerPoint presentation. All of them had cerebral palsy, which provided different challenges for each; however, they had found a way forward to become effective disability awareness presenters and advocates. The research had been focused on how they might contribute to the training of staff in order to improve home-based support. They were asked to contribute to a proposal for a new leadership skills programme by finding a name for the programme, which would convey the notion of empowered leaders capable of bringing about societal changes.

Colours and symbolic objects had been used in the brainstorm, which was then recorded on computer and displayed on a large digital wall-screen. A woman who was using a communication device indicated that she had an idea that she wanted to contribute. The message read, "yellow bird." She smiled, nodded and tilted her head to one side. The expression in her eyes suggested that there was much more to this suggestion than just the two words of "yellow" and "bird."

"Yellow bird!" It was said out loud while being transcribed.

"Oh, I get it!" said one of the other group members. "Is it the song?"

"Yes, yes!" accompanied by nodding and sounds of excitement from the contributor, as the implication of her offering had begun to be realised.

Suddenly there was spontaneous singing and humming around the room, as each had their own recall of how the song might sound:

"Yellow bird…mmm, mmm, mmm"

"Yellow bird…dit, dit, dit…."

As the lines of the song bounced around the room from different corners, it was easy to imagine someone sitting by a window and looking wistfully outside into a garden. Here they had caught sight of a colourful bird in a tree, which appeared to be alone and perhaps abandoned, mirroring the observer's own situation. On the other hand, the bird could fly away, while their own experience was one of feeling entrapped.

Our research on YouTube revealed that there were many different renditions and versions of the song, some where the language has been modernised. The most recent version included a written display of lyrics (Genius 2012). This did not include verse two of the well-known earlier version (written in the 1950s), words which were important in fully expressing the notions that the group collectively held.

How did this song speak of leadership? Although the tune was very cheerful and uplifting, the lyrics spoke of isolation, loneliness, abandonment and lack of purpose through being in a powerless position. This was how the group members had experienced their position in growing up with a disability. However, "yellow bird" could fly, could make empowered choices and was considered lucky, which had become a new part of their collective story. This was the potential of the leadership training and why the words "yellow bird" resonated as a suitable title for a leadership group.

Further research into the origins of the song has revealed that "Yellow Bird" was based on the poem "Choucoune" by Oswald Durand (1883). Michel Mauléart Monton composed music for the poem (in 1893), which was in the language of Haitian Creole (Wikipedia 2018).

Music had taken over the brainstorm session in the form of a song which had a long history of singers and musicians. For the group, the engagement in singing and exploring the "Yellow Bird" song had transformational dimensions as deeper meanings applicable to each individual were acknowledged. The song was then taken to the choir, where it was joyfully shared and further explored. A song of an archetypal nature (composed during the 1800s) had offered extraordinary metaphorical meaning over 200 years later. What was the appeal in listening to and singing "Yellow Bird"? In the final analysis, group members simply said, "Because it makes me feel happy!" "Happier, stronger and more hopeful."

Conclusion

Music is intrinsic to all of the different cultures of the world and therefore archetypal. It has the ability to engage people on multiple levels including being pleasantly immersed in the vibrations of sound, experiencing emotional connection, transforming emotional states, being a part of something bigger, being physically engaged, expressing soul, personality and identity, and being connected with memories and with "home." Music became a form of therapeutic food that brought enrichment to service users with disabilities and proved to be an essential aspect in providing multimodal arts therapy. The case studies demonstrated that music has a life of its own and can arrive in different forms to transform and extend processes in ways that are both surprising and therapeutically significant.

CHAPTER 9

Models of Supervision within the Multidisciplinary Team

Keywords: symbols, four elements, seven-foci, personalities, conflict, creative response

This chapter offers two models in supervision which are presented through case scenarios. "Seven-foci snapshots in symbols" demonstrates the use of symbols in working with the Hawkins and Shohet supervision model of seven modes (2012, p.89–111) as a successful means of providing internal supervision for interns from local and international universities. The case scenarios of Min and Jason are composites of several interns who have raised similar issues. "Conflict resolution using four elements" draws upon the Combs (2004) archetypal model of earth, water, fire and air, to offer an alternative way of working with conflict. In this, Shay, Andrea and Leaf were characters created to illustrate the supervision model in practice and are based on experiences in the roles of supervisor, supervisee and practitioner. They are also composites and do not reflect any particular persons. Both models have been applied in cases relevant to problems which can occur within multidisciplinary team (MDT) contexts. Moon (2002) stated:

> Personal therapy…and ongoing supervision are considered responsible professional practice for counselors and therapists. For the art therapist, engaging in art making as a means of self-study is an essential component…[of] professional development. Making art may be an integral aspect of supervision. (pp.58–59)

In multidisciplinary health contexts, internal supervision took place between team leader/supervisor and team member/supervisee using generic formats specific to each organisation. The purpose was to nurture the team members to grow their skills and thrive within their practices within the organisational culture and structures. The notion of supervision involving artmaking was foreign to the health contexts within the MDT. In the multimodal arts therapy service which accommodated interns, artmaking in supervision needed to be included and was extended to include a full range of creative modalities as a means of self-study and professional growth. In attending external supervision as an arts therapist, it was also important to connect with creative approaches as a means of informing the reflective process. The supervision approaches through the two models were born and raised within these particular circumstances and will be useful in a number of other contexts.

Seven-foci snapshots in symbols

The multimodal arts therapy service provided opportunities for interns and student volunteers to gain practical experience in the field. This provided a higher level of staffing beyond the allocated funding, usually allowed to assist people with physical disabilities to participate fully in groups. In describing the Montreal facility, Lister *et al.* (2011) stated:

> The Centre…has provided art, drama, music, and dance/movement therapies…with the goals of developing and enhancing self-esteem, social skills, and communication abilities. (p.34)
>
> …art and drama therapy students have obtained their practicum experiences at the center, and along with volunteers from other university departments…they ensure the center's smooth running. (p.35)

Supervision of interns occurred through co-facilitation and in designated supervision sessions. There were complexities in the way in which the supervisee/supervisor relationship functioned when compared with contexts where the supervisor was external and the two were not in a workplace relationship. It was important to establish an effective means of providing sanctuary for supervision sessions where self-reflection and new growth could be nurtured. Symbols were utilised as a quick, effective means of transition into the space with the potential for supervisees to utilise various modalities during the sessions.

Eberhart (2017) has provided the terms "attentive and open presence" and "appreciative curiosity" (p.99). In supervision, these qualities could be fostered by coming together in a shared ritual using symbols to reflect upon key questions:

- How am I feeling right now and which symbol best represents this?
- Which symbol do I choose to represent my clients?
- Which symbol do I choose to represent the organisation?

Through using a creative and playful approach with symbols, open and honest mutual sharing would arise. The space was established as one where self-exploration could safely take place. The relationship could then successfully shift to that of the supervisor holding the space for the supervisee.

Hawkins and Shohet (2012) provided a supervision model, which was recognised within health and social services, within which there is an opportunity to develop modes of practice relevant to the creative therapies, and through which the symbols process was established.

Seven foci or modes are suggested which provide a balance within supervision sessions (pp.89–111) and can be effectively adapted for the creative arts therapies:

1. Awareness toward the client: therapeutic goals, presence and engagement

2. Approaches that have been implemented by the supervisee: progress made, challenges encountered, planning further strategies

3. Understanding the client and supervisee relationship: reactions, dynamics, parallel processes

4. Interests and concerns of the supervisee: professional progress, further development, creating personal and professional well-being

5. Awareness towards the supervisory relationship: rapport, roles, boundaries

6. The supervisor being aware of their own process within supervision: transference and countertransference, alignments, disparities

7. Awareness towards the organisation and broader context: models of practice, policies, funding contracts, multidisciplinary collaborations

Hawkins and Shohet (2012) stated:

> good supervision of in-depth work with clients must involve all seven processes, although not necessarily in every session…some supervisors become habituated to using just one mode. Therefore, part of the training with this model is to help supervisors…develop an integrated balance of attention. (p.106)

Case scenarios using symbols and the seven foci

SCENARIO 1: The client and the supervisee

Min had been an intern at the rehabilitation unit for six weeks. Upon graduation she hoped to work with young people in war-torn countries where there was likely to be a high occurrence of physical disabilities. As she prepared for supervision, she was feeling uncertain about her own performance. She had experienced unexpected personal issues, which might have affected her practice.

It was a relief when her supervisor suggested that they both choose from the symbols collection and take a moment to reflect as colleagues using a creative approach (*mode 5: supervisory relationship*).

- How am I feeling right now and which symbol best represents this (mode 4: supervisee; mode 5: supervisory relationship; and mode 6: supervisor's own process)?

Min had chosen a large yellow die stating that she had experienced uncertainty about things in her personal life which had affected her confidence. Her supervisor had chosen a pink clock representing the pressure of reporting deadlines and then suggested that they both take a moment to breathe and centre themselves before continuing. Min felt more relaxed when she realised her supervisor had also experienced challenges, and her confidence increased as she focused on her breath.

- Which symbol do I choose to represent my clients (mode 1: client)?

Min presented a polystyrene star which was full of potential in what it could become. Also, each client was already a star, something that she wanted them to know. Her supervisor chose a multifaceted silver ball representing a moment of unity and transformation in a group, each participant being a part of the whole. Min experienced a sense of equality in what they had each offered and it inspired her, and her anxieties dissipated.

- Which symbol do I choose to represent the organisation (mode 7: wider workplace context)?

Min chose a woven flax bag and said she was still learning what was inside the bag, that each day had brought new things out of the bag; she sometimes felt inadequate because there was a lot she did not yet know. Her supervisor had chosen an elephant because sometimes she feared she might get trampled through organisational systems; she needed to remember to ride on the back of the elephant.

The supervisor's honesty gave Min the courage to spontaneously select a fourth symbol, a shark (mode 4: supervisee). She had experienced a personal setback, as if a shark had come along and consumed her plans. This had caused her to struggle in an individual session with a client.

- What happened with the client (mode 1: client)?

The client was making an artwork and then became upset, and Min had difficulty understanding what he was trying to tell her due to his dysarthria and emotional state. He had composed himself enough to use a spell chart to explain his experience of a misunderstanding which had left him feeling angry and powerless. Min was overcome by her own sense of powerlessness through the "shark-eaten" plans. She had not been sure how to assist the client; however, he had told her that he felt much better through talking and planned to finish his painting next session. Min plucked up the courage to say to the supervisor that she had wondered if he was testing her (mode 3: client/supervisee relationship).

Min moved into her primary modality of dance movement to explore the client's issue alongside her own reaction. The supervisor witnessed her dance which began with a sense of being stuck and powerless and then moved into expansion, rhythm and flow. The supervisor paid careful attention to her own emotional and physical reactions as she witnessed (mode 6: supervisor's own process). She reflected that Min had appeared evasive when she arrived at the session and she had also experienced a sense of powerlessness and fear of perhaps being out of her depth cross-culturally. It had been a relief when the symbol work had brought energy and flow to the session (mode 5: supervisory relationship).

- What possibilities might there be toward the next session with the client (mode 2: supervisee strategies and interventions)?

Min chose further symbols as a part of a brainstorm process and they discussed what she might do to progress beyond the feeling of "being tested by the client" (mode 3: client/supervisee relationship). Min said she would work with this further in dance independently, and that her confidence had been restored toward the next session with the client.

The case scenario of Min demonstrates how the use of symbols moved both the supervisee and supervisor into a creative space where arts therapy modalities were primary. Key questions brought about the spontaneous occurrence of the seven foci of Hawkins and Shohet (2012). The dominant foci were related to the client and the supervisee.

SCENARIO 2: The wider context

Jason was in the third year of a four-year degree, and his internship at the rehabilitation unit was for several months' duration, during which time he was expected to develop proficiency within his primary modality of art therapy. He had been assisting with the multimodal groups and was enjoying this; however, his university tutors were now suggesting that he needed to move in a different direction than that of the initial agreement with the organisation. He had made a significant investment to work overseas and was feeling confused about what he might best do. As he arrived at supervision, his supervisor sensed ambivalence and despondency. She introduced the symbols that he had used with clients and suggested that they take a creative approach to the session. He was initially hesitant; however, when he realised that she was also going to participate in the process, he agreed.

- How am I feeling right now and which symbol best represents this (mode 4: supervisee; mode 5: supervisory relationship; and mode 6: supervisor's own process)?

His supervisor broke the ice by choosing a graduation teddy bear to represent being uncertain and needing to hold an inquiring mind. Jason reciprocated by choosing two animals, a tiger and a horse, which he placed so that they were facing away from each other, stating that he felt as if he was being pulled in different directions.

- Which symbol do I choose to represent my clients (mode 1: client)?

His supervisor continued to take the lead, modelling the process. She chose a doll that unscrewed in the middle to reveal other smaller dolls within it. She stated that this reminded her of how each person holds a variety of selves at different ages. Jason picked up a range of different objects—a wax apple, tiara, doll's chair, treasure box, pirate's hat—and arranged them in a circle. His supervisor noticed a shift in his energy as he became momentarily animated. He sighed and stated that he really enjoyed working with groups and the way that group members make different contributions.

- Which symbol do I choose to represent the organisation (mode 7: wider workplace context)?

The supervisor suggested that Jason choose first and he grabbed hold of two balls, one that was spiky and the other smooth, placing them side by side. He explained that currently he was involved with two organisations wanting different things. His supervisor noticed that the tension he had been holding when he arrived returned to his face. She had chosen a box with a hinged lid stating that it represented structure and containment, and then, lifting the lid, she stated that there was also flexibility. She then expressed her curiosity about the meaning of the two balls.

Jason explained that his university had said that he needed to be more focused on his primary modality and wanted him to extend his individual caseload significantly; however, since coming to the rehabilitation unit, he realised how much he enjoyed working with groups. His university had agreed to him practicing as a co-facilitator with groups; however, three months into his internship, they had put forward this new requirement.

His supervisor suggested that he choose additional symbols to represent the different options that he might have within the situation. As he did this, he arrived at three possibilities: to ask for her help to arrive at a new caseload; to renegotiate with the university toward his involvement in multimodal groups; or to find a different organisation in which to complete his internship. He decided that he would work with the first two options simultaneously and his supervisor agreed that she would explore opportunities within the service which might assist in meeting his university requirements, while also stating that the rehabilitation unit was predominantly funded for practice with groups.

Jason left the session feeling empowered toward problem solving and discussing options. The outcome was that Jason's university came to recognise that multimodal group work would enhance his art therapy practice and agreed that his core practice could take the form of groupwork, as long as art was primary within the modalities. His supervisor asked for referrals for individual art therapy from the MDT, for people who would benefit from Jason's level of training and skill set. He led a group and continued to assist in the other multimodal groups to successfully complete his internship.

Through using the questioning technique and symbols, Jason was able to clarify a significant problem that had occurred related to mode 7 (the wider context). By also exploring mode 1 (the client), he simultaneously clarified where his interests in practice lay so that he could take this into consideration when he developed his action plan. His supervisor was able to utilise symbols in a way that facilitated Jason's supervision needs (mode 4: supervisee) and addressed those needs (mode 5: supervisory relationship). She remained aware of her own responses to Jason's mood states throughout the session which helped to inform the directions taken (mode 6: supervisor's own process).

In the case scenarios of Min and Jason, the effectiveness of using symbols in combination with key questions provided natural points of entry into the seven foci of the Hawkins and Shohet model (2012, pp.89–111), and into arts therapies modalities that were aligned with practice. This brought positive, playful, interactive dynamics to the supervision arena, and provided the required safety and sanctuary within which to self-explore, creatively experiment and collaboratively problem-solve. An accepted framework relevant to health sector requirements was utilised and, at the same time, creative modalities were established as a core part of the supervision practice for those who would become registered practitioners of the future.

Conflict resolution using four elements

MDTs have been recognised as providing significant challenges for arts therapists, who have sometimes found it difficult to fully establish their role. There has often been a sense of irreconcilable differences in relationship to the approaches and values of other team members.

Miller (2016) stated:

> Problems in teams can vary from practical concerns to deeper seated problems which are difficult to access and discuss… The arts therapist… may struggle to find a place for arts therapies and to establish respect. (p.31)

Harvey, Donovan and Lammerts Van Bueren (2016) suggested that the tensions which resulted with MDT colleagues "could have been related to different values embedded within a medical-related service and those of creative arts therapies" (p.138).

Combs (2004) has offered "multi-cultural guidance on how to confidently overcome conflict and find lasting win-win solutions" (p.xxiv) through the four archetypal elements: earth, water, air and fire (represented artistically in Figure 9.1). Macauley (2010) has stated that "Jung characterizes the four elements as archetypes, which are ideas or forms of thought emanating from the experiences of a people in such a way that they are powerfully present in the collective unconscious of individual lives" (p.66). Combs has attributed character traits to each element which can both cause conflict and provide organisational balance. By recognising and understanding the dominant elements active for each party, conflict situations can be negotiated and resolved. This has provided the basis for an effective method of supervision.

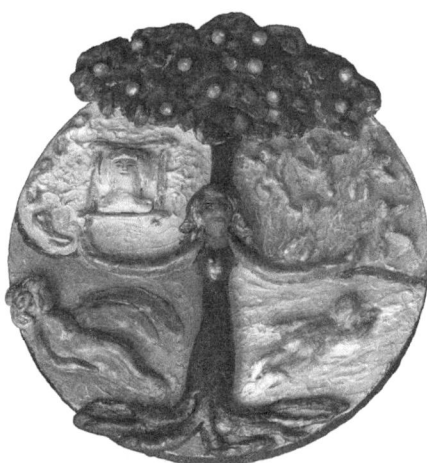

Figure 9.1 Holding the four archetypal elements (see insert for colour version)

Levey (2018), a psychologist and arts therapist, provided an experiential activity at the Auckland Fringes Art Festival 2009 in expressive dance movement, where response was invited to video projections of earth, water, air and fire. This led to personal reflections and insight for participants and demonstrated that elemental archetypes could be effectively utilised in therapeutic arts-based processes. In supervision, supervisees were encouraged to respond in the modalities/media of their choice through a flexible six-step process. Nominated steps could take place either within the session or independently for later discussion:

1. Reflect upon the four elements and key characteristics (Combs 2004) as presented in Table 9.1.

2. Produce a creative response to each within a preferred modality to discover how each element was present on an inner level.

3. Identify your own dominant archetypal element(s) within the conflict situation.

4. Identify likely dominant archetypal elements of other parties within the conflict.

5. Make a further creative response considering new insights, which clarifies the pathway forward.

6. Engage in a reflective process with the supervisor.

Table 9.1 Traits and attributes of the four elements (modified from Combs 2004)

Earth ("preserving the status quo")	Water ("adapting and avoiding conflict")	Fire ("boundless in battling for a cause")	Air ("objective, rational and unemotional")
Connected to the physical	Realm of emotions	Spirituality and creativity	Intellectual, rational thinker
Body and five senses	Sensitive, interpret as personal	Imaginative	Use structured systems: law; psychology; mathematics
Observant, notices details	Empathetic and gentle	Bigger-picture thinkers	Can lack empathy
Comfortable with the rational	Takes on the emotions of others	Unwilling to be pinned down	Can be sharp and fast-talking
Patient and diligent	Flexible and comfortable with chaos	Enthusiastic and passionate	In conflict can speak first, think later

cont.

Earth ("preserving the status quo")	Water ("adapting and avoiding conflict")	Fire ("boundless in battling for a cause")	Air ("objective, rational and unemotional")
Stoic and unmoved in crisis	Able to go with the flow	Needs acknowledgement of ideas	Loves a lively debate
Resistant to change	Conflict can cause depression	Enjoys a wild and exciting battle	Fits complex situations into applicable frameworks
Thwarts process by denying issues	Bails out of relations to avoid conflict	Frustrated rants can incite others	Articulate, willing to offer opinion
Holds grudges	Fear of hurting feelings of others	Brings life to failing projects	Great communicator and problem solver
Nurtures and grounds team or organisation	Tuned in to the moral and emotional health of groups	Cares deeply about group and its future	

Case scenarios using the four archetypal elements

SCENARIO 1: Case review within MDT setting

Arts therapist, Shay, was one year into her position with an MDT in a health context. The wider team met monthly to participate in a person-centred case review and it was her turn to present a case. Her client, Andrea, had a disability which had caused lower body paralysis and mild dysarthria, whereby her verbal articulation of some words was unclear. Through the course of her arts therapy sessions, Andrea had made new discoveries about herself, gained confidence about her prospects in life and arrived at a career goal.

Shay invited Andrea to the case review with expectations of an MDT support plan being developed; however, the clinical team leader, a registered nurse, stated that Andrea had just begun working on goals established earlier in the year and needed to complete these goals before considering new goals. Also, she had just established positive routines, and this was significant to her wellbeing. The occupational therapist suggested that Andrea's goals might sit outside of her functional capacity and needed to work on basic functional skills first.

With the support of her line manager who was also at the meeting, Shay reiterated that Andrea wanted to explore the path toward employment, a new aspirational goal that would require planning. The team then celebrated Andrea's progress, goal plans were updated and a further meeting was scheduled to discuss the required steps. Andrea seemed happy with the outcome; however, Shay was disappointed. Each time she had attended a meeting there seemed to be road blocks thrown in the way of plans.

Shay took this to her clinical supervisor who suggested that she work with an elemental archetypal approach to gain a different perspective and emotional detachment, which might promote conflict resolution. Shay read the overview of the four elemental archetypes as shown in Table 9.1. Her supervisor suggested that she respond creatively to each element in her preferred modality, and she responded with drama therapy. She took up a character for each archetype sequentially and began to hear echoes of her team members through her enactments. The occupational therapist, who had been working in the field for over 20 years, seemed to oppose any kind of changes from the established norms. She seemed reluctant to entertain new ideas, often referring to "the tried and trusted way" (earth). The clinical team leader had been instrumental in updating several recording systems and, although progressive in this way, liked things to always be approached through an established framework (air). She also saw that Andrea, the client, was a "big-picture thinker" and tended to put one idea forward and then move on to another, particularly as her disability often made it difficult to manifest the outcomes without practical assistance (fire).

Shay also recognised that she was most aligned with Andrea through being imaginative and a big picture thinker. At the same time, she was sometimes like water, wanting to run away and adapting herself to fit different situations rather than taking a stand. Through her training, she had come to recognise the value of frameworks (air). She endeavoured to keep herself well grounded and resist the tendency to rush into things (earth).

Through her progress in arts therapy, Andrea had become motivated toward her goals, and she arrived at a new aspirational goal that could potentially bring fulfilment. Shay needed to be an effective advocate at the scheduled meeting and provide the required reassurances to the other team members based on their archetypal concerns, which she role-played with her supervisor. Her shifts in thinking and insights enabled her to recognise the concerns of others in conflict situations, and she became an effective and confident negotiator in meetings and was less affected by the MDT day-to-day dynamics.

SCENARIO 2: Mobile service for residential setting

Leaf had been contracted to provide a mobile service for people who had disabilities who were living in residential settings. Each of the residences within the service held two to three purpose-built houses which accommodated six to ten people who needed 24-hour support. Although the living arrangements were established as flatting, the decision of who lived in the houses came about through a health referral process. This meant that choices of where to live and with whom to live were externally imposed. In beginning the new role, Leaf found a high level of conflict within the living situations which impacted on the formation of a positive environment for an art therapy group.

Leaf took the concerns to supervision where it was suggested that they might explore a creative archetypal approach of the four elements (earth, water, fire and air). After reading Table 9.1, Leaf could see that this approach had the potential to provide a better understanding for both self and clients, and he suggested that they would take this away to explore through a creative process. At the next supervision session, Leaf returned with a series of poems based on observations of how the archetypes were reflected within the residential context:

> **A person who wanted to stay put**
> This is the third time they've asked me if I want to change houses.
> I could get a bigger room.
> They tell me it would be better.
> But why would I want to change houses?
> This is what I know.
> These are the people I know.
> Why fix it if it's not broken? **Earth…**
>
> **A person who wanted to run away**
> Just when you get to know someone properly,
> and they finally get to know you,
> they get another job,
> or get married,
> or go overseas.
> It hurts that they are leaving,
> but no one seems to care about your feelings. **Water…**

A person who had a Pegasus chair with smoking wings on its wheels
My chair can spin like a top and speed like the wind.
It can give you a reputation for being reckless,
a danger to yourself.
Also, to pedestrians and cars.
In other circumstances,
I might have been a pilot or an aircraft engineer.
No, wait!
An astronaut looking back on the planet. **Fire…**

A person who was helping to improve the system
My flatmate is so moody.
Why can't they just accept that change is a part of life?
People come and go
but there are systems in place and they work.
It's good,
because now I am contributing to creating systems
as a volunteer advisor. **Air…**

Leaf suggested to the supervisor that they would introduce the four archetypes to people in the residential settings and invite them to also make creative responses, which the supervisor supported. An intervention was developed that involved the making of individual responses to a chosen archetype, and then of creating a group artwork that could be displayed communally. The elemental archetypes provided a means to viewing conflicts through an external framework which brought about solution-focused creativity. Residents were able to participate alongside each other with the involvement of their support staff. This began a journey toward better relationships within the residential settings and opened up new conversations within the MDT. Leaf's groups became established as a creative safety zone, and the people looked forward to their weekly visits and the creative opportunities. Moon (2002) stated:

> Most of our clients' difficulties occur in the context of relationships—with the self, others, the culture, and the environment—and so therapy must be relational and contextual in nature in order to be of benefit. From both a practical and philosophical perspective it is important that art therapy studios maintain a connection *with* the world rather than serve as a retreat from the world. (p.75)

Leaf discovered that the archetypal process facilitated an effective art therapy space within an everyday environment. Knill (2017b) stated, "All art-making requires an imaginary space that is distinct for everyday reality... [It] is, however, still part of the same world." Although there are constraints imposed by frameworks, materials and structures, "these challenges act like openings to increase the *range of play* beyond the usual one, even "beyond imagination"' (p.213). By working with the elemental archetypal framework, first for themselves in supervision and then within the residential context, Leaf was able to bring about outcomes "beyond imagination" that catalysed a process toward better living environments.

The case scenarios of Shay and Leaf explored two different conflict situations that have commonly occurred within the health and disability field. Shay found herself in conflict within the MDT which could potentially block a client's progress, and Leaf encountered conflict within residential settings which hindered the establishment of cohesive arts therapy group environments. The elemental archetypal model based on Combs (2004) was introduced through supervision and provided a framework through which their preferred creative tools of practice could be utilised, which catalysed positive shifts in perspectives and abilities. This in turn had an influence on the MDT setting which led to a better-informed environment for people who had physical disabilities.

Conclusion

Supervision is an integral aspect of working within an MDT in the health field and can be a significant aspect of the arts therapist role. The supervision provided needs to effectively meet different needs and situations, and to reflect our tools of practice which are the creative arts modalities. The supervision models of Hawkins and Shohet (2012) and Combs (2004) offered two quite different frameworks which could be approached through the archetypal and journeyed into using creative tools of choice. They both promoted a playful, interactive approach that invited solutions to arise through unconscious processes, and in which the supervisor held a supportive, collaborative position. They have been offered as a means of effectively entering the realms of archetypal creativity and arriving at positive outcomes.

CHAPTER 10

Conclusion

In providing multimodal arts therapies for people who had disabilities throughout the course of a seven-year period, archetypal approaches were recognised as offering effective points of entry into the imaginal realm which catalysed growth and positive changes. Archetypes were provided in the form of archetypal cards, symbols and mythological stories, and also arose in unplanned forms through responding to the therapeutic process, where an archetypal approach presented as a relevant and effective way forward. This led to engagement in a diverse range of approaches that are recognised as being archetypal including through rituals and notions of the ancient worlds.

There were reasons to ponder Jungian ideas of the collective unconscious, individuation, animus and representations of Self through mandala and other symbolic objects. Archetypal approaches proved particularly significant where physical mobility and verbal communication were limited, while the imagination was expansive and could provide a form of liberation. Meaning making in therapy was held as being within the rights and capabilities of participants. The engagement with the unconscious through the use of archetypes in the creative modes of art, dance, drama and music in individual and group sessions brought about therapeutic outcomes relevant to measurable personal goals.

Arts therapy took place within a multidisciplinary setting and there was a strong sense of community in the way that this was provided. Initiatives were supported and sometimes instigated at management level to be assisted by the wider team. The success of arts therapy groups was dependent upon additional assistance, which included support staff, interns and volunteers. This led to the need for effective supervision methods which were aligned with the multimodal arts therapy approaches, examples of which have been included.

The role of the arts therapist was one of being a companion who was privileged to share in the creative journeys and stories of inspirational people. It is through their generosity, and their desire to both be recognised in their wholeness and to make a difference in the lives of others, that this book has been written.

References

Aluede, C. and Aiwuyo, V. (2002) "Ethnomusicologists and Medical Practitioners in Healthcare Delivery in Nigeria." In G. Emeagwali and E. Shizha (eds) *African Indigenous Knowledge and Sciences: Journeys into the Past and Present*. Rotterdam: Sense Publishers.

Arrien, A. (1992) *Signs of Life: The Five Universal Shapes and How to Use Them*. New York: Tarcher/Putnam.

Baum, F. (2016) *The New Public Health*. Melbourne: Oxford University Press.

Bly, R. (2002) "Three Views of the Shadow." In M.R. Waldman (ed.) *Shadow: Searching for the Hidden Self. Archetypes of the Collective Unconscious, 1; Reflecting American Culture Through American Literature and Art*. New York: Tarcher/Putnam.

Bolen, J. (1985) *Goddesses in Every Woman: A New Psychology for Women*. New York: Harper Colophon.

Bruscia, K. (1991) *Case Studies in Music Therapy*. Gilsum: Barcelona Publishers.

Buetow, S., Talmage, A., McCann, C., Fogg, L. and Purdy, S. (2014) "Conceptualizing how group singing may enhance quality of life with Parkinson's disease." *Disability and Rehabilitation 36*, 5, 430–433.

Bunt, L. and Hoskyns, S. (eds) (2002) *The Handbook of Music Therapy*. London: Routledge.

Campbell, D. (1992) *Music and Miracles*. London: Quest Books.

Campbell, J. (1976) *Creative Mythology: The Masks of God*. New York: Penguin Books.

Cameron, J. (1997) *The Vein of Gold: The Journey to Your Creative Heart*. New York: Pan Books.

Chodorow, J. (1997) *Jung on Active Imagination*. Princeton, New Jersey: Princeton University Press.

Combs, D. (2004) *The Way of Conflict: Elemental Wisdom for Resolving Disputes and Transcending Differences*. Navato, California: New World Library.

Council, T. and Phlegar, K. (2013) "Cultural Crossroads: Considerations in Medical Art Therapy." In P. Howie, S. Prasad and J. Kristel (eds) *Using Art Therapy with Diverse Populations: Crossing Cultures and Abilities*. London: Jessica Kingsley Publishers.

Csordas, T. (1999) "Embodiment and Cultural Phenomenology." In G. Weiss and H. Haber (eds) *Perspectives on Embodiment: The Intersections of Nature and Culture*. New York: Routledge.

Durie, M. (2001) *Mauri Ora: The Dynamics of Maori Health*. Melbourne: Oxford University Press.

Eberhart, H. (2017) "The Arts Work: The Process of Intermodal Decentering in Professional Conversations." In E. Levine and S. Levine (eds) *New Developments in Expressive Arts Therapy: The Play of Poiesis.* London: Jessica Kingsley Publishers.

Ellis, R. (2001) "Movement metaphor as mediator: A model for dance/movement therapy process." *The Arts in Psychotherapy 28,* 181–190.

Estes, C. (1992) *Women Who Run with Wolves: Myths and Stories of the Wild Women Archetype.* Toronto: The Random House Publishing.

Evans, B. (2015) "Reflections on mandala-making in nature." *Australia and New Zealand Journal of Arts Therapy 10,* 1, 80–81.

Fabjanski, M. and Brymer, E. (2017) "Enhancing health and wellbeing through immersion in nature: A conceptual perspective combining stoic and Buddhist perspectives." *Frontiers in Psychology 8,* article 1573. Accessed on 27/02/2018 at www.frontiersin.org

Feen-Calligan, H., McIntyre, B. and Sands-Goldstein, M. (2011) "Art therapy application of dolls in grief recovery, identity and community service." *Art Therapy 26,* 4, 167–173.

Friedman, H. and Mitchell, R. (eds) (2008) *Supervision of Sandplay Therapy.* Hove: Routledge.

Genius (2012) *Yellow Bird: The Sapphires Soundtrack.* Accessed on 24/02/2018 at https://genius.com/Jessica-mauboy-yellow-bird-lyrics

Glassman, E. (2013) "Giving Teens a Visual Voice: Art Therapy in a Public School Setting with Emotionally Disabled Students." In P. Howie, S. Prasad and J. Kristel (eds) *Using Art Therapy with Diverse Populations: Crossing Cultures and Abilities.* London: Jessica Kingsley Publishers.

Gnatt, L. (2013) "Stories Without Words: A Cultural Understanding of Trauma and Abuse." In P. Howie, S. Prasad and J. Kristel (eds) *Using Art Therapy with Diverse Populations: Crossing Cultures and Abilities.* London: Jessica Kingsley Publishers.

Goldsworthy, A. (1990) *A Collaboration with Nature.* New York: H.N. Abrams.

Gombrich, E. (1979) *The Story of Art.* Oxford: Phaidon Press.

Gordon-Flower, M. (2014a) "Nursing the wounded heart." In C. Miller (ed.) *Assessment and Outcomes in the Art Therapies: A Person-centred Approach.* London: Jessica Kingsley Publishers.

Gordon-Flower, M. (2014b) "Dancing with the magic of the archetypes." In C. Miller (ed.) *Assessment and Outcomes in the Art Therapies: A Person-centred Approach.* London: Jessica Kingsley Publishers.

Gordon-Flower, M. (2016) "Dances of paradox and role diffusion." In C. Miller (ed.) *Arts Therapists in Multidisciplinary Settings: Working Together for Better Outcomes.* London: Jessica Kingsley Publishers.

Granot, A., Regev, D. and Snir, S. (2017) "Jungian theory and its uses in art therapy in the viewpoints of Israeli arts therapists." *International Journal of Art Therapy 23,* 2, 1–12.

Halprin, D. and Weller, J. (2003) *The Expressive Body in Life, Art, and Therapy: Working with Movement, Metaphor, and Meaning.* London: Jessica Kingsley Publishers.

Harvey, S., Donovan, J. and Lammerts Van Bueren, T. (2016) "Considerations of Change in Play Therapy with Young Children." In C. Miller (ed.) *Arts Therapists in Multidisciplinary Settings: Working Together for Better Outcomes.* London: Jessica Kingsley Publishers.

Hawkins, P. and Shohet, R. (2012) *Supervision in the Helping Professions.* Maidenhead: Open University Press/McGraw-Hill.

Hill, M. (1997) *Nature Works: Sculptures in the Landscapes.* Auckland: Godwit Publishing.
Ho, R. (2017) *Arts: It's All About Beauty, Abilities, and Endless Possibilities.* TEDxWanChaiSalon, YouTube. Accessed on 30/09/17 at https://www.youtube.com/watch?v=Fb1T7qiMdxs
Hosli, E. and Wanzeried, P. (2017) "Education on the Edge: Acts of Balance." In E. Levine and S. Levine (eds) *New Developments in Expressive Arts Therapy: The Play of Poiesis.* London: Jessica Kingsley Publishers.
Howie, P., Prasad, S. and Kristel, J. (eds) (2013) *Using Art Therapy with Diverse Populations: Crossing Cultures and Abilities.* London: Jessica Kingsley Publishers.
Jung, C. (1964) *Man and His Symbols.* New York: Doubleday.
Kalff, D. (2003) *Sandplay: A Psychotherapeutic Approach to the Psyche.* Cloverdale, California: Temenos Press.
Knill, P. (2017a) "The Essence in a Therapeutic Process: An Alternative Experience of Worlding." In E. Levine and S. Levine (eds) *New Developments in Expressive Arts Therapy: The Play of Poiesis.* London: Jessica Kingsley Publishers.
Knill, P. (2017b) "Community Art: Communal Art-Making to Build a Sense of Coherence." In E. Levine and S. Levine (eds) *New Developments in Expressive Arts Therapy: The Play of Poiesis.* London: Jessica Kingsley Publishers.
Knill, P., Levine, E. and Levine, S. (2005) *Principles and Practices of Expressive Art Therapy: Toward a Therapeutic Aesthetics.* London: Jessica Kingsley Publishers.
Landy, R. (2009) "Role Theory and the Role Method of Drama Therapy." In D. Johnson and R. Emunah (eds) *Current Approaches in Drama Therapy.* Springfield, Illinois: Charles C. Thomas Publishers.
Lem, A. (1993) *Music Therapy Collection: Introducing the Principles and Objectives of Music Therapy Practice in Australia.* Canberra: Australian Dance Council – Ausdance (ACT).
Levey, A. (2018) "Projects: Golden Doors." Accessed on 30/12/2018 at http://www.alleviate.co.nz/#projects
Levine, S. (2017) "Aesthetic Education: Learning Through the Arts." In E. Levine and S. Levine (eds) *New Developments in Expressive Arts Therapy: The Play of Poiesis.* London: Jessica Kingsley Publishers.
Levine, E. and Levine, S. (2017) (eds) *New Developments in Expressive Arts Therapy: The Play of Poiesis.* London: Jessica Kingsley Publishers.
Lewis, P. (1996) "Depth psychotherapy in dance/movement therapy." *American Journal of Dance Therapy 18,* 2, 95–113.
Lister, S., Tanguay, D., Snow, S. and D'Amico, M. (2011) "Development of creative arts therapies centre for people with developmental disabilities." *Art Therapy 26,* 1, 34–37.
Lubin, H. and Johnson, D. (2008) *Trauma-Centred Group Psychotherapy for Women: A Clinician's Manual.* New York: Psychology Press.
Macauley, D. (2010) *Elemental Philosophy: Earth, Water, Air and Fire as Environmental Ideas.* New York: Suny Press.
Majid, N. (2010) *My Mother Was the Earth, My Father Was the Sky.* Oxford: Peter Lang.
Manaia, A. (2017) "Kaupapa Māori arts therapy: The application of arts therapy in a Kaupapa Māori setting." *Australia and New Zealand Journal of Arts Therapy 12,* 1, 29–39.
McAdams, D. (1993) *Stories We Live By: Personal Myths and the Making of the Self.* New York: William Morrow.

McNiff, S. (1992) *Art as Medicine: Creating a Therapy of the Imagination.* Boston, Massachusetts: Shambhala Publications.

McNiff, S. (2004) *Art Heals: How Creativity Cures the Soul.* Boston, Massachusetts: Shambhala Publications.

McNiff, S. (2017) "Cultivating Imagination." In E. Levine and S. Levine (eds) *New Developments in Expressive Arts Therapy: The Play of Poiesis.* London: Jessica Kingsley Publishers.

Meeus, W., Iedema, J., Maassen, G. and Engels, R. (2005) "Separation-individuation revisited: On the interplay of parent-adolescent relations, identity and emotional adjustment in adolescence." *Journal of Adolescence 28*, 89–106.

Merchant, J. (2009) "A reappraisal of archetype theory and its implications for theory and practice." *Journal of Analytical Psychology 54*, 339–358.

Miller, C. (ed.) (2016) *Arts Therapists in Multidisciplinary Settings: Working Together for Better Outcomes.* London: Jessica Kingsley Publishers.

Mitchell, S. (1994) "Reflections on Dramatherapy as Initiation Through Ritual Theatre." In Jennings, S., Cattanach, A., Mitchell, S., Chesner, A. and Meldrum, B. (eds) *The Handbook of Drama Therapy.* New York: Routledge.

Moon, C. (2002) *Studio Art Therapy: Cultivating the Artist Identity in the Art Therapist.* London: Jessica Kingsley Publishers.

Myss, C. (2003) *Archetype Cards and Guidebook.* London: Hay House.

Nordoff, P. and Robbins, C. (1971) *Therapy in Music for Handicapped Children.* London: Victor Gollancz.

Pearson, C. (1991) *Awakening the Heroes Within: Twelve Archetypes to Help Us Find Ourselves and Transform Our World.* New York: Harper Collins Publishers.

Roberts, M. (2017) "Touching the earth: Creating steps towards re-establishing a connection with nature." *Australia and New Zealand Journal of Arts Therapy 12*, 1, 20–28.

Roesler, C. (2012) "Are archetypes transmitted more by culture than biology? Questions arising from conceptualization of archetypes." *Journal of Analytical Psychology 57*, 223–246.

Rothschild, B. (2000) *The Body Remembers: The Psychophysiology of Trauma and Trauma Treatment.* New York: W.W. Norton.

Ryan, R. and Deci, E. (2001) "On happiness and human potentials: A review of research on hedonic and eudaimonic wellbeing." *Annual Reviews Psychology 52*, 141–166.

Scategni, W. (2015) *Psychodrama, Group Processes and Dreams: Archetypal Images of Individuation.* London: Routledge.

Schlaug, G. Marchina, S. and Norton, A. (2008) "From singing to speaking: Why singing may lead to recovery of expressive language function in patients with Broca's aphasia." *Music Percept 25*, 4, 315–323.

Sepinuck, T. (2013) *Theatre of Witness: Finding the Medicine in Stories of Suffering, Transformation, and Peace.* London: Jessica Kingsley Publishers.

Siemon, M. (1980) "The separation-individuation process in adult twins." *American Journal of Psychotherapy XXXIV*, 3, 387–400.

Sobol, B. and Howie, P. (2013) "Cultural Considerations in Family Art Therapy." In P. Howie, S. Prasad and J. Kristel (eds) *Using Art Therapy with Diverse Populations: Crossing Cultures and Abilities.* London: Jessica Kingsley Publishers.

Stace, S. (2014) 'Therapeutic doll making in art psychotherapy for complex trauma.' *Art Therapy 31*, 1, 12–20.

Swallow, M. (2002) "The Brain – Its Music and Its Emotion: The Neurology of Trauma." In J. Sutton (ed.) *Music, Music Therapy and Trauma: International Perspectives.* London: Jessica Kingsley Publishers.

Turner, B. (ed.) (2017) *The Routledge International Handbook of Sandplay Therapy.* New York: Routledge.

Virtue, D. (2004) *Goddess Guidance Oracle Cards: A 44-Card Deck with Guidebook.* London: Hay House.

von Franz, M. (1999) *Archetypal Dimensions of the Psyche.* Boston, Massachusetts: Shambhala.

Walker, B. (1988) *The Women's Dictionary of Symbols and Sacred Objects.* New York: Harper & Row.

Weinrib, E. (2004) *Images of the Self.* Cloverdale, California: Temenos Press.

Weiten, W. (2004) *Psychology Themes & Variations.* London: Wadsworth.

West, W. (2011) "Spirituality and Therapy: The Tensions and Possibilities." In W. West (ed.) *Exploring Therapy, Spirituality and Healing.* New York: Palgrave Macmillan.

Whitaker, P. (2017) "Art Therapy and Environment (*Art-thérapie et environnement*)." *Canadian Art Therapy Association Journal 30*, 1, 1–3.

(2004) "Māori Legends: New Zealand in History." Batman Ed. 4. *The New Zealand Encyclopaedia.* Accessed on 11/02/2018 at http://history-nz.org/maori9.html.

(2018) "Choucoune." *Wikipedia.* Accessed on 24/02/2018 at https://en.wikipedia.org/wiki/Choucoune_(song).

(2018) "What is the mysterium Tremendum et Fascinans?" *Encyclopaedia Britannica.* Accessed on 04/01/18 at https://www.britannica.com/topic/mysterium-tremendum-et-fascinans.

Further Reading

Elder, H. (2017) "Te Waka Kuaka and Te Waka Oranga. Working with Whānau to improve outcomes." *Australian and New Zealand Journal of Family Therapy 38*, 27–42. doi: 10.1002/anzf.1206.

Garlock, L. (2016) "Stories in the cloth: Art therapy and narrative textiles." *Art Therapy 33*, 2, 58–66.

Houkamau, C. and Sibley, C. (2010) "The multi-dimensional model of Māori identity and cultural engagement." *New Zealand Journal of Psychology 39*, 1, 8–28.

Kalmanowitz, D. and Ho, R. (2016) "Out of our mind: Art therapy and mindfulness with refugees, political violence and trauma." *The Arts in Psychotherapy 49*, 57–63.

Kapitan, L., Litell, M. and Torres, A. (2011) "Creative art therapy in a community's participatory research and social transformation." *Art Therapy 28*, 2, 64–73.

Kidd, J. and Wix, L. (2013) "Images of the heart: Archetypal imagery in therapeutic artwork." *Art Therapy 13*, 2, 108–113.

Knox, J. (1999) "The relevance of attachment theory to a contemporary Jungian view of the internal world: internal working models, implicit memory and internal objects." *Journal of Analytical Psychology 44*, 511–530.

Schlaug, G., Marchina, S. and Norton, A. (2010) "From singing to speaking: Why singing may lead to recovery of expressive language function in patients with Broca's aphasia." *National Institutes of Health – Public Access Authors Manuscript, Music Precept 25*, 4, 315–323.

Sezaki, S. and Bloomgarden, J. (2011) "Homebased art therapy for older adults." *Art Therapy 17*, 4, 283–290.

Index

aesthetic responsibility 49
Aiwuyo, V. 138
Aluede, C. 138
ancient civilisations 50–9
animus 45
Archetypal Cards 118
archetypal concepts 15–6
archetype, definition 15–6
Around the World Through the Seasons dance 105–15
Arrien, A. 78, 80, 85, 88, 93
artefacts creation 52–7
Arts Therapy 5-Pt Star Model
  aesthetic skills domain 30
  case study 27–31
  international research study on 24
  lifestyle development domain 30
  overview 22–4
  relationships domain 29
  self-evaluation form 24
  self-reflection domain 29
  and symbols combined 26–31
  transformational engagement domain 29

Baum, F. 19, 20
Bly, R. 128
Bolen, J. 60
Bruscia, K. 135
Brymer, E. 79, 85
Buetow, S. 133
Bunt, L. 135, 136, 137

Cameron, J. 85, 86, 91, 93, 141
Campbell, D. 135, 138
Campbell, J. 61
canoes, waka 68–9
case studies
  ancient civilisations 50–9
  Around the World Through the Seasons 105–15
  Arts Therapy 5-Pt Star Model 27–31
  drama of *The International Convention of the Pacific* 124–31
  drama of *The King-Knight's Daughter* 118–24
  environmental sculpture 83–4
  fairy gardens 40–7
  goddess dolls 59–68
  Legends of Maui dance 98–105
  sacred vessels 68–76
  social story board 32–40
  supervision using symbols 147–51
  Time-Life-Lines 86–90
  Voices of the Māori gods (music) 137–41
  "Yellow Bird" song 141–3
Chinese New Year 69
Chodorow, J. 16
client group 13–4
collectivism 104
Combs, D. 152, 153, 158
communal art-making 76
conflict resolution using four elements 151–8
conscious/unconscious in opposition 16
Councill, T. 21

Csordas, T. 97
cultural context 17–8, 125–8

dance movement
　case study: Around the World Through the Seasons 105–15
　case study: Legends of Maui 98–105
　choosing songs 106–7
　developing choreographed movement 96
　embodiment in 97–8
　and making artworks 96–7
　in multidisciplinary team context 94–5
　public performance 98
　warm-ups 95–6
day-by-day inquiry 15
Deci, E. 79
Diwali 69
dolls
　goddess dolls 59–68
　historical roles of 59–60
　naming 65
Donovan, J. 152
drama
　case study: The International Convention of the Pacific 124–31
　case study: The King-Knight's Daughter 118–24
　overview of group 116–8
　role-taking 117
Durie, M. 136

Eberhart, H. 146
elements, four archetypal 152–8
Ellis, R. 97
embodiment 97–8
Encyclopaedia Britannica 61
environmental sculpture
　background 78
　benefits of 79
　case study 83–4
　Intervention in Nature process 80–2
　labyrinths 90–3
　Time-Life-Lines 85–90
Erikson, Erik 44
Estes, C. 78, 85, 86, 91, 93
Evans, B. 78, 79, 85

Fabjanski, M. 79, 85
fairies 44
fairy gardens 40–7
family patterns, generational 21
Feen-Calligan, H. 59, 60, 61
"fight-or-flight" option 21
four archetypal elements 152–8
Friedman, H. 25

generational family patterns 21
Genius 142
Glassman, E. 20
Gnatt, L. 21
goal-setting
　Arts Therapy 5-Pt Star Model 26–31
　goddess dolls 66–7
goddess dolls 59–68
Goddess Guidance Oracle Cards 61–2
Goldsworthy, A. 78
Gombrich, E. 58
Gordon-Flower, M. 22, 24, 60, 61, 63, 95, 97
Granot, A. 18, 25
grief, "stuckness" in 34–5
group unconscious 18

Halprin, D. 95, 97
Harvey, S. 152
Hawkins, P. 144, 146, 147, 149, 151, 158
hieroglyphic symbols 51
Hill, M. 78
Ho, R. 19
holistic approach 14
Hoskyns, S. 135, 136, 137
Hosli, E. 50
Howie, P. 20, 21
humanist approach 136

individuation 45
"Instinctual Trauma Response" 21
Intervention in Nature process 80–2

Johnson, D. 30, 33, 85
Jung, C. 16, 17, 45, 59, 99, 116, 123, 130, 131

Kalff, D. 84
Knill, P. 16, 25, 37, 76, 157
Kristel, J. 20

labyrinths 90–3
Lammerts Van Bueren, T. 152
Landy, R. 117
Legends of Maui dance 98–105
Lem, A. 135
Levey, A. 152
Levine, E. 25
Levine, S. 25, 49
Lewis, P. 95, 97
limitations (in approaches applied) 18
Lister, S. 145
Lubin, H. 33, 39, 85

McAdams, D. 33, 36, 44
Macauley, D. 152
McIntyre, B. 59, 60
McNiff, S. 16, 25, 46, 84, 90
Majid, N. 98
Manaia, A. 136
mandala 84
Marchina, S. 137
Maui, Legends of 98–105
Meeus, W. 45
mentors 39
Merchant, J. 17
methodology 15, 17
Miller, C. 151
Mitchell, S. 118
Mitchelle, R. 25
mixed-media artwork 42, 52
Moon, C. 62, 144, 157
multicultural context 17–8, 125–8
multimodal approach 14
music
    archetypal nature of 132, 135
    case study: Voices of the Māori gods
        137–41
    case study: "Yellow Bird" 141–3
    choirs 133–4
    in multimodal arts therapy groups
        135–7
    music therapy spectrum 136
    percussion 134
    singing by non-verbal clients 137
    songs for dance movement 107

Myss, C. 26, 28, 116, 117, 118, 124
mythology, functions of 61

naming (of dolls) 65
nature see environmental sculpture
non-verbal clients 19
Nordoff, P. 135
Norton, A. 137

painting 41–2
Pearson, C. 37
personal unconscious 18
Phlegar, K. 21
pop-up vision boards 47
poverty 19–20
practise-based inquiry 15
Prasad, S. 20
public performance 98

Regev, D. 18
relationships map 35–6
ritual ceremony 37–8
Robbins, C. 135
Roberts, M. 78
Roesler, C. 15, 16
role-taking 117
    see also drama
Rothschild, B. 33, 85, 91
Ryan, R. 79

sacred vessels 68–76
Sandplay therapy 25
Sands-Goldstein, M. 59, 60
Scategni, W. 16
Schlaug, G. 137
sculpture
    of sacred vessels 71–5
    see also environmental sculpture
seasons archetypes 105–14
self-evaluation form 24
Sepinuck, T. 98
shadow side 124, 128, 130–1
shapes, archetypal 80
Shohet, R. 144, 146, 147, 149, 151, 158
Siemon, M. 46
singing see music
site of trauma 91
Snir, S. 18

Sobol, B. 21
social story board 32–40
spirituality 69
Stace, S. 63
stress, chronic 19–20
supervision
   importance of 144–5
   seven modes model 146–7
   using four elements in 151–8
   using symbols in 145–51
Swallow, M. 135
symbolic realm 97
symbols
   and Arts Therapy 5-Pt Star combined 26–31
   in individual and group therapy 24–6

Te Whare Tapa Whā 136
Time-Life-Lines 85–90
trauma, site of 91
Turner, B. 84
twins 46

unconscious
   four levels of 18
   in opposition with conscious 16
universal unconscious 18

Virtue, D. 61
von Franz, M. 16, 18

waka canoes 68–9
Walker, B. 57
Wanzeried, P. 50
Weinrib, E. 84
Weiten, W. 44, 104, 113
Weller, J. 95, 97
West, W. 69
Whitaker, P 78
Wikipedia 142

"Yellow Bird" song 141–3